STOP MARKETING, START BELONGING.

DESIREE MARTINEZ

STOP MARKETING, START BELONGING.

REAL-WORLD MARKETING THAT BUILDS LOYAL CUSTOMERS ANYWHERE

KAST
MEDIA
GROUP

For information, address Kast Media Group,
a publishing imprint of Pink Media Inc.,
Brighton, Michigan.

www.mrsdesireerose.com

Library of Congress Cataloging-in-Publication Data is available upon request.

ISBN 979-8-218-85599-4 (paperback)
ISBN 979-8-218-85610-6 (ebook)

Bulk purchases for promotional, educational, or business use are available.
For more information, please contact Kast Media Group.

First Edition: 2026

To all the small towns that prove
belonging is built, not found.

Especially to the one I get to call home.
Brighton, Michigan, thank you for opening your arms,
cheering for my work, and holding my family in a way no
place ever has.

To Stephen.
You have backed every dream, every reinvention,
and every leap. Your belief in me has never
wavered, and it is the reason I could
write this book and do anything.

You are where I belong.

Table of Contents

Prologue

"Where are you from?"

For most people, that's an easy question. They can point to a city or a small town and be done with it.

For me? It has never been that simple. I grew up a military kid and then became a military spouse, which means I'm from nowhere and everywhere all at once. When someone asks me that question, my brain immediately wants to follow up with, "Well, what exactly do you mean? Do you mean where I live now? Where I was born? Where I've lived the longest? The place I liked best? The place on my driver's license?"

Like I said, it's never been an easy answer.

But here's what I've learned: being from nowhere and everywhere shapes you into a very particular kind of person.

You get good at walking into brand-new places, knowing absolutely no one, and figuring out how to make them feel like yours. You learn to adapt quickly, read people fast, and figure out the unspoken rules of a community.

It also leaves you with this itch. A curiosity about people and places and how communities actually work. When you've had to start over again and again, you start looking for the fastest way to connect. You want to know what makes this place tick.

When you grow up moving every few years, you figure out pretty quickly that if you want to feel at home, you can't wait for people to come to you. You've got to jump in with both feet. You try the food, learn the customs, show up to the quirky traditions. That's how you move from living in a place to living with it.

I learned that lesson everywhere we went.

In Japan, I was amazed at how a million people could share such a small island and still move with this calm, steady rhythm. Okinawa is only about 10 miles wide and 70 miles long, yet life ran smoothly because people dedicated themselves fully to whatever they were doing.

In Korea, we squeezed every drop out of each of the four seasons. We ate street food like it was our job, went to festivals, and even spent a weekend studying Buddhism with a monk. Do you know how many bows you do in a weekend like that? A hundred and six. I know because I did them, counting with a bracelet I made just to keep track.

Back in the States, the pattern continued.

In Florida, we only had ten weeks, so I went full force into finding every unique, can't-find-it-anywhere-else spot to eat. There was one place that literally threw rolls at you. Another Italian restaurant that, to this day, is still some of the best pasta I've ever had. And the Gulf Coast? Warm water and sand so soft it felt like flour slipping through your fingers.

In Texas, we made it a mission to see everything. Big cities. Fairs. Festivals. Food. Austin had the best Renaissance Festival we've ever been to, and I still order Jank's barbecue sauce because nothing else compares.

Everywhere we went, the lesson was the same: you can't just live in a place. You have to live with it.

After years of moving, diving into new communities, and making the most of every assignment, we hit a point where we thought: maybe it's time to find our forever home.

For a hot minute, we dreamed about becoming full-time RVers. Cruising across the country, pulling into small towns, and just knowing when we'd found "the place." But the more we thought about it, the more we realized that lifestyle might look adventurous, but it doesn't let you put down roots.

So we went with familiarity.

For us, that meant Phoenix. We had family there. Old friends. We knew the city and the neighborhoods. It felt like a safer choice than starting over yet again.

But once we got there, reality set in. The city was noisy and expensive. The heat made summer a punishment. And hardest of all we were disconnected from the very people we thought would be our foundation. The love was still there, but our lives had moved in different directions. Conversations didn't flow the same. The connection just wasn't there anymore.

And then COVID hit.

Whatever small momentum we had toward building community vanished overnight. Lockdowns shut everything down. Suddenly, it was clear: we were alone.

The turning point came during a trip to visit friends in Seattle. For the first time, we watched our kids play outside in the summer. A simple thing, but a huge shift for us. Neighbors knew each other. People gathered outside. Kids roamed between houses. It was a glimpse of something we'd been missing all along.

That's when we knew. It was time to move.

But where?

Instead of throwing darts at a map, we made a list. We wanted affordability, shared values, and multi-generational longevity, the kind of place people don't just pass through but stay. Our research pointed to the Midwest. Minnesota. Wisconsin. Michigan.

And then it hit me: Michigan wasn't just on the list because of data. It was personal.

My dad was from here. When I think back on my rootless childhood, Michigan is the closest thing I had to a home base. We always circled back here for holidays and family visits. We even lived here for a few years when my dad went to the University of Michigan after his time in the Marines. So Michigan wasn't just logical, it was familiar. And in the middle of so much change, familiarity felt right.

Once we decided, the move happened fast. Three weeks. We sold our house, packed a truck, loaded our camper and car with two kids, three dogs, two bunnies, and all our hopes for a fresh start, and drove across the country.

When we landed here, everything felt different. Not perfect, just…human.

The town wasn't just a grid of houses and stores. It had personality. A once-a-year melon ice cream tradition that brings everyone together. A high school mascot that unites the whole town. A tiny movie theater where the entire audience claps in sync before every film.

These weren't quirks. They were signals of belonging.

That's when it clicked. The same things I'd been doing my whole life to connect personally were the same things that make businesses thrive locally.

It's not about being the loudest. It's not about showing up first on Google. It's about becoming part of the heartbeat of your community.

When I started growing my business here, I realized I couldn't rely only on my online audience from YouTube or social media. I had to build the way this town builds: through people.

Not funnels. Not cold outreach. Not whatever tactic is trending this week.

So when a neighbor told me about a local BNI chapter, I showed up. Not because I was desperate for leads, but because recommendations matter here. Word of mouth carries weight. And if someone you trust says, "You need to meet these people," you listen.

From the very first meeting, I knew it was different. The vibe was warm. People laughed, swapped personal updates before business ones, and teased each other like old friends. Business wasn't ignored, it just wasn't the only thing. Relationships came first. And because of that, business flowed naturally.

That's what so many people online get wrong. They think visibility is the same as success. They chase follower counts and views, but that's not what builds loyalty. People don't do business with you just because you popped up first. They do business with you because they trust you, believe you care, and know you'll solve their problem.

That's the connection. That's the "aha." And it's the blueprint for building a business that lasts.

Because whether you're running a bakery, a law firm, a landscaping company, or a marketing agency, growth always comes back to the same thing: real people, real relationships, real trust. And as our marketing world becomes more automated, more AI-driven, and more impersonal, those human connections are only going to matter more. The more technology takes over, the more people crave in-person experiences and micro-communities where they feel seen.

That's why marketing is really about building community. It's not about shouting the loudest or throwing money around hoping people notice you. It's about showing up, learning the rhythms, joining the traditions, and proving you care. Just like a town welcomes you when you lean in, your customers welcome you when they see that you're not just here for the transaction, you're here for the long haul.

And that's what this book is about.

It's not a theory, a gimmick, or a quick-fix promise. It's a guide for building a marketing approach that actually works in the real world, with real people, in real communities both offline and online. Because marketing isn't two separate worlds. It's both.

It's the conversation you have at a Chamber lunch and the follow-up email that keeps the connection alive. It's sponsoring the local Little League and being the first result when a parent Googles your service. It's the flyer someone picks up at a street fair and the Instagram post that reminds them of you later.

Too many business owners treat those things like they're separate. They're not. They're all connected. And when you learn to make those pieces work together, something powerful happens: your customers don't just see your business, they recognize you as part of their community.

This book will show you how to do that.

Here's how it works:

- First, we'll look at how your marketing shows up today and where it feels scattered, disconnected, or overly transactional, so you can see what's actually helping you build trust and what's just noise.

- Then, we'll ground everything in the human side of your business. Your story, your values, and the people you serve, because community can't be built without clarity on who you are and why you exist.

- Next, we'll modernize the traditional things that already work. Networking, events, print, sponsorships, and in-person relationships, and show you how to update them for how people connect today. Then we'll connect those efforts to digital tools like email, social, video, and search so your relationships do not stop when the event ends or the handshake does.

- Finally, we'll bring it all together into a way of marketing you can actually sustain. One that feels natural, human, and aligned with how you already do business. One that builds trust over time, supports your growth, and helps your business become part of the community it serves instead of just another option people scroll past.

Here's the truth: whether you run a service business, a shop on Main Street, a consulting practice, a small agency, or a long-established company, growth comes back to the same foundation: real people, real relationships, real trust.

This book is going to help you stop treating offline and online like two separate worlds. The truth is, your business needs both: the traditional, face-to-face ways people have always built trust, and the digital tools that keep those relationships alive between handshakes.

We're going to take what actually works in the real world: networking, events, print, sponsorships, those community-driven tactics that have always mattered, and update them for how people connect today. Then we'll show you how to bridge those refreshed, in-person strategies with the digital world of email, social, video, and search. Not in silos, but as one living, breathing system that makes your marketing human again with modern updates based on how people are peopling these days.

By the end, you won't just have a list of tips. You'll have a blueprint for weaving together the best of both worlds: the warmth of traditional marketing with the reach and consistency of digital. That's how you build belonging, not just visibility. That's how your business becomes more than another name in the feed; it becomes part of your customer's world.

Because when you stop marketing and start belonging, your business doesn't just get noticed - it becomes part of something bigger.

Chapter 1:
Stop Doing Random Acts of Marketing

Sharon walks into her office on a Tuesday morning ready to tackle her client files. As a veteran estate planning lawyer in New York, she has built her reputation on helping families in Brooklyn and Manhattan navigate one of the most sensitive and important areas of their lives. She's good at what she does. That's why clients trust her.

But about 45 minutes into her focused work session, her inbox dings. It's an email from the advertising service that has been her main source of leads for years. They need updated ad copy by tomorrow or her campaign pauses. Sharon sighs, closes the brief she was working on, and starts hunting for the right words. She isn't a marketer, a copywriter, or a designer. She's a lawyer. Still, she spends the next hour drafting copy, fiddling with the graphic, and emailing it back before it's too late.

Finally, she gets back to her casework. But not long after, another alert pops up. Her social media management tool needs to be reconnected to Facebook or her posts won't publish. She logs in, tries to reconnect, and gets sucked into her feed: friends' vacation photos, political rants, random updates she never planned to see. Ten minutes of distraction later, she remembers the case file sitting open on her desk.

By the afternoon, she's back on track,until her calendar pings with another reminder. It's time to write the weekly email to her list. Her only problem? She has no idea what to say. Should she send an article? A reminder? A story? She knows she should email regularly, but she stares at the blank screen, frustrated and uncertain. So, she just doesn't do it and gets back to her case files.

This is Sharon's normal. She runs her firm. She manages her staff. She handles client work. And she also juggles all the marketing, whether she wants to or not.

Here's the kicker: Sharon isn't unusual.

This is the reality for most small business owners. They end up spending 80% of their time trying to figure out how to market their business when they would rather spend 80% of their time doing the thing they went into business to do.

The result? They end up cobbling things together, learning on the fly, feeling like they're always behind, and ultimately don't do most of the things they need or want to do.

Ignoring The Problem

Sharon's situation isn't unique. Almost every business owner I've worked with is living a version of the same story. They're not just running the business they dreamed of — they're running two full-time jobs. The first is the job they signed up for: practicing law, fixing cars, cutting hair, training clients, building houses, baking bread. The second is the job they didn't sign up for but can't escape: marketing.

And the truth is, most business owners don't do the second job well, not because they aren't capable, but because they're already exhausted by the first.

So what happens? They stop doing it.

They don't send an email asking for a Google review after a job, even though those five-star ratings could double their referrals. They don't follow up with past clients, so repeat business slips through the cracks. They leave their outdated website online because "it works fine" — never mind that it loads slowly, buries the contact form, and gives no real reason to choose them over anyone else. They post three times on Facebook in a month, nobody calls, and they decide social media is a waste of time.

The reasons are endless: not enough time, not enough knowledge, trying once and giving up, or simply not seeing the value.

And here's where it gets interesting: when people don't understand marketing, they mock it.

My husband is brilliant. The kind of person who dives deep into whatever fascinates him, whether it's history, politics, or science. As a kid, whenever he'd share what he'd learned with adults, they'd cut him off, make a joke, or wave him away. Not because he was wrong, but because they didn't understand. It was easier to dismiss him than to engage with something unfamiliar.

That's exactly what happens with marketing. People dismiss what they don't get.

They roll their eyes at "those kids on TikTok." They grumble about the emails in their inbox and decide they'd never want to "spam" people with one. They tell themselves networking is pointless because they're introverts and no one would talk to them anyway.

I've lived this firsthand. I've been in social media marketing since MySpace. I built my career on helping businesses grow online, and even after six years of making a living from "posting on Facebook," my extended family would ask when I was going to get a "real job." It wasn't until I bought a house — eleven years into running my own business — that my dad finally stopped worrying about what I did for a living.

But here's the thing: dismissing marketing doesn't make it go away. It just makes you invisible. And invisibility is the fastest way to lose in business.

Random Acts of Marketing

Marketing gets overwhelming fast. Everywhere you look, someone is shouting that the thing you have been doing for years is "dead" and their shiny new product is the only answer. At networking events, in your inbox, on social media, the pitches never stop. And they all sound good because the people selling them are good marketers.

That is how so many business owners end up with what I call random acts of marketing.

- You sponsor the Little League team because some- one asked, but you do not have a plan to connect that sponsorship back to your business.

- You buy a print ad that blasts your message to every- one in town, even though your ideal customer is only a fraction of that audience.

- You drop a couple thousand dollars on Google ads while the agency "tests" and you wonder where the money went.

- You go to a networking mixer only to realize halfway through that none of the people in the room are your actual demographic.

None of these things are bad. In fact, they can all work. But when you do them in isolation, with no plan to connect or follow up, they become expensive distractions. You end up busy but not effective.

That is why so many business owners throw up their hands and say, "I've tried everything and nothing works."

And the twist: even when you do find something that works, like a networking group, repeat referrals, or posting on Face- book, if you rely on that one thing forever it will eventual- ly plateau.

Even the most tried-and-true tactics evolve. I remember being in a BNI group in 2012 where everything was tracked

24 : *Stop Marketing, Start Belonging*

on paper slips. Fast forward to today, and there is an app that not only tracks referrals but connects you with members across the world. The principle has not changed. You still need to show up, give value, and build relationships. The tools, however, have advanced.

Which brings us to the real truth: there is no single, perfect marketing strategy.

Two lawyers in the same city, serving the same clients, can have completely different approaches that work. Two plumbers offering the exact same services will market differently if one is in a small town and the other is in a big metro. The rhythms of the community, the demographics, the owner's own personality and comfort level all shape what will actually work for you.

That is why copying someone else's "perfect formula" never feels right. Marketing is not about doing everything. It is about building the right foundation and then adapting it to fit your business, your audience, and you.

From Random to Belonging

When my family moved to Michigan, I thought I had marketing figured out.

By that point, I had been on YouTube since 2017, I had built a strong digital presence, and during COVID, my business had its biggest glow-up yet. I was educating business owners online, running everything from my office in pajama pants and a professional top, rocking the business mullet life. I had a website, a YouTube channel, an email list, social media accounts, and I was even speaking on stages around the country.

From the outside, it looked like everything was working. But something was missing.

I wasn't connected to my town. People didn't know me. I had all the digital pieces, but without the human layer, it didn't convert into belonging.

That realization hit me the first time I walked into a local BNI meeting. Suddenly, things clicked. I met people who solved my problems immediately, like finding a new insurance agent after mine moved away without telling me. By the second meeting, I already had a referral for my business.

But here's the key: it wasn't just because I showed up once. It was because I stayed visible between those meetings. I put members on my email list. I shared videos that proved my expertise. I posted on social media and tagged their businesses when I could. By the time I walked into that room again, I wasn't just a new face anymore — I was someone they had already seen online, someone they could trust to do what I said I could do.

That referral turned into a long-term client who still works with me today as their fractional CMO. Not because I made the perfect elevator pitch, but because the in-person connection and the digital proof worked together.

And that's the gap I see everywhere.

Some businesses are like I was — heavy on digital, but invisible locally. Others do the opposite — they network in person, sponsor events, and rely on referrals, but have no digital foundation to back it up. In both cases, the result is the same: random acts of marketing that never connect, never scale, and never feel sustainable.

That's why belonging matters.

Belonging is what happens when you intentionally integrate the traditional and the digital. It's not just about having all the pieces. It's about making them work together in a way that fits who you are, how you serve, and where your customers are.

When you belong, your marketing stops being random. It starts becoming a working system.

Where We're Going

This book isn't about giving you one more shiny tactic to try. You've already done that. You've sponsored the thing, bought the ad, posted on Facebook, maybe even hired someone to "do your SEO." And if you're honest, you've probably felt the same frustration Sharon felt: busy, but not moving forward.

Here's the shift.

The businesses that win — the ones that grow, thrive, and stay trusted — don't rely on random acts of marketing. They build systems that connect.

And that's exactly what we're going to do in these pages.

1. Modernize traditional marketing practices:

   We're going to take the old-school things you've seen work — networking, sponsorships, partnerships, print, events — and update them for today. Not by replacing them, but by showing you how to make them more intentional, more measurable, and more human.

2. Build nurturing systems online:

   We'll layer in the digital tools that let you stay visible even when you're not in the room. Emails, social posts, video, reviews, websites — not as separate silos, but as extensions of your real-world relationships.

3. Create a cycle of belonging that scales:

   When the traditional and the digital start talking to each other, your marketing stops being random and starts becoming a loop. You show up, you nurture, you scale, and the cycle repeats. That's how you build not just visibility, but loyalty. That's how you stop chasing tactics and start building a business people remember, recommend, and return to.

This is the formula at the heart of the book:

$$\text{Traditional Marketing} + \text{Digital Nurturing} = \text{Scaled, Trusted Business.}$$

By the time you're done reading, you'll not only understand the why, but you'll have a framework to do it — your way, in your voice, in your community.

Your Starting Point

Before we go any further, pause and take a quick audit of where you are right now.

Grab a notebook, the notes app on your phone, or even the margin of this page — and answer these four questions honestly:

1. What have you done to market your business in the past year?

2. Which of those things actually brought you customers, and which ones didn't move the needle?

3. What's one thing you've been meaning to try but haven't started?

4. What's one thing you know you should be doing, but you've stopped (or never do consistently)?

You don't need perfect answers. This isn't a test. It's about seeing your reality in black and white.

Because here's the truth: most of what you've done isn't "wrong." It's just disconnected. The point of this book is not to shame you for past attempts or pile more tactics onto your plate. The point is to take what you've already done — the networking, the sponsorships, the partnerships, the ads, the content — and plug them into a system that actually works.

Bringing It Home

You've already been doing pieces of this. You've already taken action. The frustration you've felt is not because you're lazy, or because you're bad at marketing. It's because no one has shown you how to connect the dots.

This book will.

We're going to modernize the traditional practices that have always worked. We're going to layer in digital nurturing that keeps your business visible and memorable. And we're going to build a cycle of belonging that scales, so you stop relying on random acts of marketing and start building a business that thrives.

You don't have to do everything. You just have to do the right things, consistently, and in a way that feels authentic to you.

That's how you go from invisible to unforgettable. That's how you build a business people trust, recommend, and return to.

It all starts with you choosing to stop spinning your wheels and start building belonging.

So grab your pen for note taking (each chapter has a 'Your Takeaways' spot for you to take notes), look at where you are, and take action now.

Be on the look out for Digital Drops.

These are short, punchy pieces of digital strategy you can plug directly into your marketing. Think of it like a small but mighty delivery: a drop of tech, tools, or tactics that integrates with your traditional marketing.

Each "Digital Drop" is designed to be quick to understand, easy to apply, and powerful enough to move the needle without overwhelming you.

Your Takeaways

What were your takeaways from this chapter?

_____

_____

_____

_____

What real-world or in-person action will you take because of this chapter?

_____

_____

_____

_____

What digital action will you take to support or extend that effort?

_____

_____

_____

_____

Chapter 2:
Let's PLANT a Garden

When I hit my late thirties, I decided it was time to pick up an "old lady hobby." I had options: knitting, bread making, gardening. Lucky for my family, I picked all three. I've got the chunky yarn blankets all over my house, a sourdough starter named Frank, and a patio garden that makes me way happier than I ever expected.

Now, I could stretch this into some clever metaphor about knitting or sourdough, but gardening is the one that stuck AND it's the one that has the best marketing connection and visuals.

One of the best things about moving to Michigan is that everyone here grows something. You can drive down almost any road in the summer and find tables at the end of driveways loaded with vegetables, flowers, or eggs. You drop cash in a box or Venmo the number on the sign and head home with food that was growing just hours ago.

That was not my reality in Arizona. I tried to garden there, but it was brutal. Three hundred plus days of sun and weeks of triple-digit heat meant I spent more time trying to keep plants alive than actually enjoying them. Shade cloth, constant watering, moving pots in and out. It was exhausting and discouraging.

Michigan flipped the script. The soil is rich, the weather is balanced, and the growing season actually lets you enjoy the process. Suddenly, I had tomatoes filling baskets, potatoes I could dig with my kids, and even a lemon bush named Luna that I haul inside during the winter.

Here is the thing about gardening. It takes effort, but it pays you back. You start with a seed, you nurture it, and before long you are turning fresh tomatoes into pizza sauce that tastes better than anything you could buy.

That is how marketing should feel. Too often, it feels like Arizona: hot, dry, and frustrating, with nothing surviving. But when you treat it like Michigan, when you understand the ecosystem and tend it with intention, it actually grows. It produces something real you can harvest.

That is what this chapter is about. The PLANT framework will show you how to prepare, launch, nurture, refine, and track your marketing so it grows into something sustainable. Just like a garden, belonging in your business does not happen by accident.

You have to PLANT it.

How the PLANT Framework Works

Before we dive into each piece of the PLANT framework, we need to talk about why it works and why we always start where we start.

Once upon a time, a business's "home base" was obvious. It was the storefront. It was the office. It was the business card you handed out or the logo on your sign. People knew you because of where you were and how you showed up.

Today, your home base is your website.

Your website is the headquarters of your business. Period.

It is the one thing that has stayed relevant for more than twenty-five years while platforms and trends have risen and fallen. The tools have changed, but the purpose has not. It is still the one place you own, the one place you control, and the one place where all your marketing should lead.

Think about it. No matter what kind of marketing you are doing - print, networking, social media, ads, sponsorships, PR - the goal is to send people to your website. Why? Because that is where everything lives.

- It is where people figure out who you are and what you do.
- It is where they see reviews and proof you can actually deliver.
- It is where they can buy from you, fill out a form, or grab your number.

- It is where you can tag them with a cookie so you stay visible long after their first visit.

- It is what helps you show up higher in search when people are ready to buy.

Your website is the home base of your business. And honestly, when someone tells me they are struggling to grow but their site is outdated, confusing, or missing altogether, it makes sense.

Now, I could spend an entire book walking you through the details of design, load times, security, and navigation. But this is not that book. This is not a manual. This is a guide. My job is to help you see what belongs together and why so you can finally stop throwing money and time at random tactics that never connect.

That is why we start with the website. That is why it is the first step in PLANT. Because until you have a digital home base, every other marketing effort is like tossing seeds on concrete.

Digital Drop:

If you need help with the details of how a website should work and all the other how-tos that connect to this book, bring it to The Table. That is our community where you can finally stop doing random acts of marketing and start learning the small but powerful steps that make the whole system work. www.mrsdesireerose.com/TheTable

The PLANT Framework

P – Prepare the Soil (Website Foundation)

Nothing grows in bad soil. You can buy the fanciest seeds, water them every day, and sing them love songs, but if the dirt is dry and lifeless, nothing is sprouting. That is your website.

Your website is not just a pretty online brochure. It is the home base that feeds Every. Single. Marketing. Effort.

It has to be alive, clear, and ready for action. It should do these three things right away:

1. Be fast!

2. Explain the problem you are going to solve for them.

3. Make it obvious how to get started.

People's expectations of a website are vast and all subconscious. They want no interference with their scrolling while simultaneously wanting it all laid out in front of them at the speed of light. They don't want to do too much. (And honestly, they don't want to have to think too much either.)

They just want their problem solved and they come to you hoping that you will be that answer.

In order to be that solution for them, we want to enrich your website with all the good nutrients that will allow for your business to blossom for your potential customers. We need to include: SEO, reviews, opt-ins, information, FAQs, calls to action, pictures & videos, shopping or scheduling links, tracking tools, links to your social media sites, blog posts jam packed with all the things they could ever want to know about your business or industry, and also it needs to be pretty.

When you get the soil right, you are giving your seeds every chance of not just surviving but thriving.

L – Launch Seeds (Marketing Initiatives)

Now we need to plant some seeds in that sexy, nutrient-rich soil you put all kinds of thought, time, and money into. You worked hard to prepare your website. You don't just want to throw any old seed in there and hope for the best. You want the right seeds — the ones that will launch your garden into abundance and success.

So what kind of seeds should you plant?

Seeds are your big, intentional marketing efforts. These are not the little extras like a one-off social post or a flyer taped to the coffee shop bulletin board. Seeds are the heavy hitters that anchor everything else. Think:

- A networking group you actually commit to showing up for.
- A sponsorship that puts you in front of the right audience.
- A podcast or YouTube channel where you build authority.
- A campaign around a product launch or seasonal push.

Not all seeds are created equal, and not every seed is right for your business. Some require constant care. Others practically grow themselves.

Take tomatoes. They are divas. They need pollinators, wind, 8–12 hours of sun, extra support structures, pruning, and just the right balance of water. Too much and you'll get nothing but stems. Too little and they shrivel.

Potatoes? Totally different vibe. You drop them in the dirt, water them occasionally, and let them do their thing. Both tomatoes and potatoes can feed you, but they require very different levels of time and attention.

Your marketing seeds are the same. Some efforts need you to show up constantly with energy, resources, and follow-through. Others keep growing quietly in the background with a lot less effort. Neither is good or bad — but you need to pick based on your budget, your bandwidth, and your ability to sustain them.

You do not want to plant more than you can handle. If you scatter seeds everywhere without the ability to care for them, you are setting yourself up for a garden full of sad, half-grown plants. It is better to choose one seed you are willing to learn about, nurture, and give your time to than to overwhelm yourself with too many you cannot manage.

When I first started gardening, I grew one tomato plant in a container on my porch. That one plant taught me everything: what to do, what not to do, and how to recover when I messed up. I panic-Googled things like "why are my tomato leaves yellow," "why is my plant tall but not sprouting flowers," and "why are my tomato bottoms brown." I fell into gardening TikTok and learned about nitrogen, watering less but better, and even the trick of having bumblebees nibble your plants to simulate pollen activity. I tried things. I adjusted. I over-pruned. I cut off entire stems by accident. I killed more tomatoes than I want to admit when I went out of town.

But by the end of the season, I still had a basket full of tomatoes that made a few jars of the best sauce of my life. And the next season? I grew even more.

Your marketing is the same. It is better to pick one seed you are willing to learn about, nurture, and give real time to than to overwhelm yourself with too many you cannot handle.

So what seed do you pick?

The rest of this book is full of updated, modernized traditional and digital practices that will help you decide. As you go, you'll see which seeds make sense for your business, which ones fit your comfort level, and which ones align with your goals and audience.

When you launch the right seeds, you are giving your marketing garden the best chance to grow because you've chosen the ones that match your capacity and commitment.

A – Activate Nurturing (Digital Feeding)

Don't be fooled. Those seeds are not just going to grow on their own.

You can plant the perfect seed in the richest soil, but if you walk away and never water it, never give it light, never check on it, you are not going to get much more than a patch of dirt and disappointment.

This is where most people mess up. They think once the seeds are in the ground, the work is done. Wrong. Seeds need feeding. They need consistency. They need a reason to keep pushing roots down and sprouting up.

Marketing works the same way. Once you have chosen your main seeds, you cannot set them and forget them. You have to nurture them. That means showing up, giving them attention, and building the habits that keep them alive.

And let's be real, nurturing is not glamorous. It is not the shiny "launch day" excitement. It is the day-in, day-out routine. It is the watering, the checking, the adjusting. It is dealing with bad weather and droughts. It is animals stealing your harvest or bugs moving in because you made your plant such a great place to be. It is ordinary, steady work that makes the extraordinary results possible.

Your big, intentional marketing efforts require big plant energy. We are talking weekly email newsletters that keep you top of mind, carousel and vertical videos on social that actually get watched, ads directing people back to your beautiful website, mailers hitting your target neighborhoods, sponsoring the local sports ball event with a giant QR code plastered across your banner, even hosting a dinner where your network gets to hear about your latest initiative. It's all the little things layered together that drive traffic and build those bridges between your brand and the problem you solve for your customer.

When you consistently feed your seeds, you create the rhythm that turns potential into growth. Without it, all you have is fancy dirt with nothing to show for it.

Digital Drop: The New Seven Times

You may have heard the old idea that someone needs to see your brand seven times before they buy. That rule is outdated. In today's digital world, it often takes twenty or more meaningful touchpoints before someone feels ready to work with you. That does not mean creating twenty different things.

It means repurposing intentionally. One strong piece of content can become many touchpoints across email, social, and conversation. Repurposing is not about doing more work. It is about letting your best work show up often enough to build trust, familiarity, and momentum.

One seed. Many chances to grow.

N – Nix the Weeds (Audit and Refine)

Every garden has weeds. They pop up fast, they look harmless at first, and before you know it they are stealing all the nutrients your plants need to survive. If you do not deal with them, they will choke out everything you worked so hard to grow.

Marketing weeds show up the same way. They are those little things that creep into your calendar or your budget and convince you they are important. A random ad you boosted because a platform told you to. A networking event you keep going to even though nobody there is ever going to hire you. An old flyer that still has a QR code leading to nowhere. All weeds.

And the thing about weeds is that sometimes they look green and healthy. Sometimes they trick you into thinking they are doing something useful just because they are growing. But they are not feeding you. They are stealing from the seeds you intentionally planted.

This step is about getting honest with yourself. What is working? What is just keeping you busy? What do you need to rip out so your strong efforts can thrive?

Now, I am not saying you can never experiment. Some weeds might turn out to be wildflowers, and that is fine. But if you are drowning in marketing tasks, chances are your business is overrun with weeds. Pulling them frees up your time, your money, and your energy for the seeds that actually produce results.

The truth is most businesses are not struggling because they are not doing enough. They are struggling because they are doing too much of the wrong stuff.

T – Track the Harvest (Measure Results)

When you grow a garden, you do it because you want to eat. But the harvest is not just the final tomato you slice or the potatoes you roast for dinner. A healthy garden gives you so much more along the way. The blossoms attract bees, hummingbirds, and butterflies. Those pollinators help your plants produce more fruit. Sometimes they even spread seeds to new spots you didn't expect.

Marketing works the same way.

Most people think of marketing as a straight line: I did this one thing, and I got this exact amount of money back. That is a very narrow way to measure success. Marketing is bigger than that. It is sales, yes, but it is also attention, influence, impact, reputation, and referrals. It supports your sales team, it keeps your brand top of mind, and it builds trust in your community.

So when you measure your marketing, you are not just asking, "Did this ad bring in dollars today?" You are also asking:

- Did this sponsorship show people that my business is a trusted part of the community?
- Did my weekly social posts keep me visible even if nobody bought right this second?
- Did my emails stay in front of past clients so they think of me first when they need me again?
- Did my consistency give me more referrals, more word of mouth, more conversations?

These are the pollinators of your marketing. They do not always show up as an instant sale, but they create the conditions for sales to happen again and again.

Tracking your harvest means looking at all of it — the sales, the referrals, the opens, the clicks, the comments, the visibility, the attention. All the ways your work is paying off. Some will be direct. Some will be ripple effects. Together, they are how you know your garden is thriving.

Because the point of planting and nurturing seeds is not just to get one tomato today. It is to create an ecosystem that feeds you season after season.

Bringing PLANT Together

The PLANT framework is your system for turning random acts of marketing into an ecosystem that actually works.

- P – Prepare the Soil: Build a strong website foundation that can feed every marketing effort.

- L – Launch Seeds: Choose the big, intentional efforts that anchor your strategy.

- A – Activate Nurturing: Feed those seeds consistently with the steady work that makes them grow.

- N – Nix the Weeds: Pull out the distractions that choke your results and waste your energy.

- T – Track the Harvest: Measure results. Not just sales, but all the ripple effects that show your garden is thriving.

When you use PLANT, your marketing stops being Arizona — dry, frustrating, and barely surviving — and becomes Michigan, where the soil is rich, the system is balanced, and the harvest actually shows up.

Now what?

The PLANT framework is not about doing more, it is about doing what matters and knowing how each piece connects. It is the guide that takes the guesswork out of marketing and gives you a clear, repeatable way to build belonging with your audience.

Now that you know the system, the next question is simple: what seeds are you going to plant? This book is filled with updated, modernized marketing practices — both traditional and digital — that you can pick from. Think of each one as a seed packet. You will decide which ones fit your soil, your time, and your goals, and then you will know how to nurture them inside the PLANT framework.

And just like a garden, this work is not only about the harvest. Gardens bring people together. They give us flowers to smell, food to share, beauty to enjoy, and a sense of peace that makes us feel safe and welcome. Businesses can do the same thing. We are naturally drawn to the shops with flowers out front, the café with herbs growing by the window, the spaces that feel alive. Those touches make us want to step in and stay awhile.

That is the power of PLANT. Your marketing is not just about getting attention. It is about creating an ecosystem where the right people feel invited, cared for, and connected. When you pick the right seeds and nurture them with intention, you are not only growing your business, you are growing belonging.

So now it is time to choose your seeds, do the work, and build the ecosystem your audience wants to be part of.

Your Takeaways

What were your takeaways from this chapter?

_____

_____

_____

_____

What real-world or in-person action will you take because of this chapter?

_____

_____

_____

_____

What digital action will you take to support or extend that effort?

_____

_____

_____

_____

Chapter 3:
Print Marketing

I hate getting mail. Nothing makes me roll my eyes faster than opening my mailbox to a stack of envelopes I never asked for. Insurance offers, credit card pitches, refinancing letters. I could wallpaper my whole house with the amount of junk that gets stuffed into that tiny little box. The only piece I actually look forward to is what I call my "magic mail." It is from a small creator I found on Instagram who hooked me with a clever reel. Now, every month, I get to go to magic school by mail. Hogwarts never sent my letter, but this is close enough.

The problem is not that mail exists. The problem is that most of it is irrelevant, unmemorable, and wasteful. There are actual decluttering hacks that tell you to sort your mail while standing over the trash because you already know that is where most of it will end up. And if that is where your marketing lands, you are not just losing attention. You are literally throwing money away.

It is not just mail. Physical marketing shows up everywhere. Billboards litter the skyline on highways, giant signs shout at us from buildings, and every commute is filled with messages fighting for space in our brains. Some of them are digital, some are static, but most of them are forgettable. Then there is conference swag. I tell people not to hand me stuff because I know it is going straight in the trash. I do not need more pens. I do not need another tote bag. I definitely do not need another cheap notebook

This would obviously lead you to believe that print marketing is a waste of time, but that is not the case. Print marketing done badly is a waste of time and a literal waste of money. Print marketing that creates a memorable experience for people is something that will always be valuable. Rather than letting our print marketing be noise, what if we focused instead on creating experiences people actually want to keep? It is better to spend $100 on five really good pieces that stick with someone and turn them into a customer, than to spend $100 spraying and praying that something might convert.

I have seen this firsthand. One of my favorite examples is a piece of swag I got from Sendible, a social media tool I have loved and used since the early 2010s. At Social Media Marketing World in 2019, they handed out a small phone stand. Nothing flashy, just a simple, sturdy stand branded with their logo. To this day it sits in my bathroom, holding my phone while I get ready. It has propped up countless audiobooks, streamed YouTube videos, and supported endless selfie videos that I have shared on social media. It is useful, intentional, and connected to a brand I already trusted. That is what good print marketing should feel like.

And sometimes, it is the simplest things that last the longest. Like mugs. (But not coffee mugs. Coffee is gross. Keep that dark, soul-sucking bean juice far away from me and out of my cups.) Give me a proper tea mug. A big one. Sixteen ounces or bust. A tea mug is something I will keep, use, and associate that brand with positive vibes with every cup of tea I drink.

Print marketing is not the problem. How you use it is. On its own, print can easily become noise. But when it is intentional and part of a larger system, it becomes a strong tool for creating connection and belonging with your target customer.

Branding vs Marketing (Where Print Fits)

Most businesses confuse branding with marketing. They slap their logo on a pen, a tote bag, or a billboard and call it "branding." But branding is not about putting your name on as many surfaces as possible. Branding is about identity, trust, and story — who you are and how people feel when they see your name. Marketing is the system that carries that identity into the world, across every channel, and turns it into results.

This is where Sandie Cortez's perspective comes in. Sandie has run First Impressions Print and Marketing for more than 30 years. She has seen every fad and shift in marketing, from fax machines to Facebook, and one thing she repeats over and over is that print works when it reflects the brand and supports the system around it. A postcard is not just a postcard. A banner is not just a banner. They are touchpoints in a bigger web of connection.

Sandie has watched countless businesses waste money on random acts of marketing — ordering a pile of flyers because it was "cheap" or putting their name on giveaways that nobody wants. Those pieces end up in the trash, and so does that money. But she has also seen print transform businesses when it is intentional. When the print piece matches the brand's colors, fonts, and story. When the QR code drives people to the right place online. When the same campaign is echoed on social media and email. That is branding and marketing working together.

A perfect example of intentional print marketing starts at the Howell Melon Festival. The Howell Melon Festival is an iconic tradition that has been running for more than 40 years in Howell, Michigan. It celebrates a special variety of melon that grows only in that region, and every year the whole town comes together for a festival, vendors, and plenty of melon to eat.

The highlight is a limited-run batch of melon ice cream made by the local Rotary in partnership with Guernsey Dairy. They sell out every single year. Families line up, pre-orders disappear within weeks, and the ice cream becomes the centerpiece of the county's summer memories. I know when I bring home a gallon of melon ice cream, my kids can't get enough of it.

Hartland Insurance has been a part of the community since the early 80s (we will learn more about them in the next chapter). They wanted to do more than just slap their logo on a banner and call it a day. Instead, they asked: how do we become part of the actual experience?

Their answer was simple but brilliant.

You cannot enjoy the festival's signature ice cream without scooping a ball of that creamsicle colored dairy goodness. So Hartland Insurance handed out branded ice cream scoops to go along with the ice cream sold at the festival. It was intentional. It was practical. And it tied their name to a tradition the community treasures.

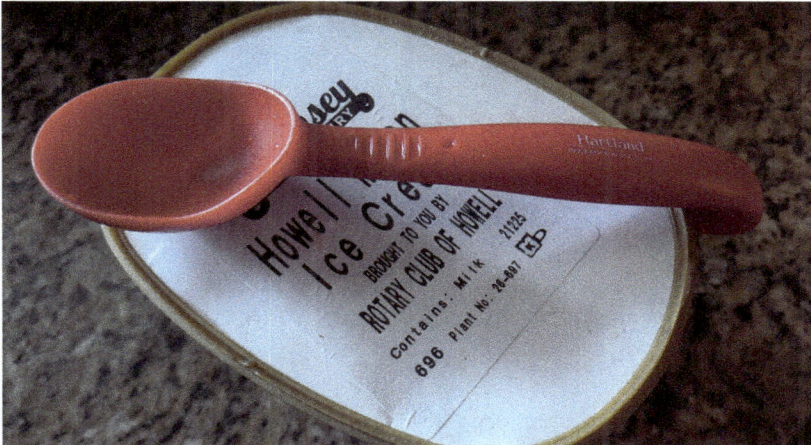

Legendary Howell Ice Cream with the Hartland Insurance scoop.

That is the difference between random acts of marketing and true belonging. People do not remember a banner. They remember who gave them the scoop they used to serve up melon ice cream on a hot summer night. Hartland Insurance became part of the memory, part of the story, and part of the tradition.

That is branding and belonging. Connecting to your community in a memorable and intentional way. When branding and marketing are aligned, print becomes more than paper and ink. It becomes a tangible experience that connects your story to your customer's life.

From Bad to Belonging

When print is intentional, it does more than deliver a message. It creates a moment. Whether it's an ice cream scoop at a local festival or a phone stand from a brand you trust, great print marketing sticks. It earns attention. It becomes part of the customer's story.

But let's be honest. Most businesses aren't doing it right. They either go too broad (sending generic flyers that mean nothing to the person opening them) or they throw money at swag and hope something lands. That's not a strategy. That's noise.

There is one simple truth about print marketing: print works if you work it right.

To make this easy for you, I organized them into Five Rules for Print That Works. These core principles will separate bad print from print that builds trust, tells a story, and drives real results.

These aren't gimmicks. They're the real-world rules for how to make your print marketing part of a system that builds belonging, not just awareness. Use these to gut-check your current materials or as a guide to create something new. And yes, we'll talk about how digital fits into all of it too.

Five Rules For Print That Works

Rule #1: Consistency Is Non-Negotiable

If your print looks different from your website, your social media, or your storefront, you've already lost. In today's noisy world, brand confusion is brand death.

When someone sees your print piece, they're asking: Is this really you? And if the fonts, colors, or messaging don't match what they've seen online or in person, even subconsciously, they don't trust it. They ignore it. Worst case, they throw it out.

This doesn't mean every single thing has to be identical, but it must feel like it belongs to the same brand family. Your postcards should echo your homepage. Your brochures should carry the same tone and promise that your social captions do. Your flyers should lead to a landing page that doesn't feel like a bait and switch.

You want people to feel like they know you the moment they see something from you. Your print marketing should never feel like a stranger.

A great example of this in real life is Precision Comfort, a heating and cooling business that doesn't just throw out random postcards hoping something sticks. Their whole approach is built on consistency. Every single piece — the mailers that hit your mailbox, the ads in the local newspaper, the signs in yards — all match. Same colors. Same fonts. Same logo. Same layout. It's easy to recognize because they've made it easy to recognize.

And they don't stop there. Every postcard includes a specific call to action and a QR code that takes people to a dedicated page on their website. Not a homepage. Not a generic link. A focused destination that lines up with the message they're sending. That's how you make your print work. You build trust and familiarity through repetition, and you guide people exactly where you want them to go.

Take Action Now

If you want your print to actually work, you need to stop winging it and start documenting your brand. Every business — yes, even small service-based businesses — should have a brand guide.

Here's what goes in it:

- Your logo in all versions (horizontal, stacked, color, black and white, transparent)
- Your brand colors with hex codes or CMYK values
- Your fonts (both header and body)
- Logo usage rules (Where can it go? What background colors are allowed? Should it ever be stretched, flipped, or squished? Spoiler: No.)
- Your brand voice and tone (Are you conversational? Buttoned-up? Casual but smart? Write it down.)

This isn't fluff. This is about being prepared. When someone on your team wants to make a flyer, or you hire a local print shop to design a door hanger, you hand them the brand guide and say: "Use this." No guessing. No inconsistencies. No confusion.

Digital Drop: Create Your Brand Guide

Use Adobe Express to build a simple brand guide with your logo, colors, fonts, and voice. Save it, share it, and use it every time you make a print piece so everything stays consistent.

mrsdesireerose.com/BrandGuide

Rule #2: Print Needs a Purpose

If you're just printing things to "get your name out there," stop. That's not purpose. That's a panic move.

Your print piece isn't a billboard for your ego. It's a tool. A tool should do something: start a conversation, bring someone to your store, drive a scan, create a memory, or spark a sale. When it has no purpose, it has no power. It just becomes more noise for people to ignore.

Here's the question you should ask every single time you plan a print piece:

"What exactly do I want this to do?"

That might mean:

- A table tent at a restaurant asking diners to leave a Google review

- A door hanger reminding neighbors about your seasonal service
- A direct mailer offering a discount that brings people into your store
- A business card that starts a follow-up funnel

The point is that it should do something specific. Not everything has to sell right away, but everything should lead somewhere: to connection, to conversation, to conversion.

Print is not the end of the marketing. It's a stepping stone. Make sure yours leads somewhere worth going.

Precision Comfort doesn't just send out pretty mailers. They plan their print with clear goals in mind. Every postcard is tied to a specific offer, a seasonal need, and a target neighborhood. In the fall, their glossy, high-quality mailers remind homeowners to schedule HVAC maintenance before Michigan's freezing temps kick in. In the spring, they follow up for AC tune-ups, giving customers a second chance to take action. Each piece has a job to do: not just to be seen, but to drive the next step.

That's purposeful print.

Rule #3: Design Like You Mean It

We're living in the goldfish era. According to a Netflix study, it takes about 1.5 seconds for a viewer to decide to watch a show or scroll right past. That same instinct applies to your marketing. If your design looks cluttered, chaotic, or homemade, people won't take you or your business seriously.

Good design builds credibility. It makes people stop, look, and believe you're worth their time.

We've all seen bad design: business cards with six fonts, postcards crammed edge to edge with text, flyers printed on cheap paper with blurry logos and awkward cuts. That's not just ugly. It screams, "I didn't care enough to do this right." Even big brands get lazy and send out stuff that feels dated or sloppy. But for small businesses, every piece counts.

Clean layout. Legible fonts. Modern colors. Quality materials. These are not "nice to haves." They are non-negotiables if you want to earn attention and keep it. You don't need fancy. You need to be intentional. Less noise. More clarity.

Back to Precision Comfort: their mailers are thick, glossy, and clear. There's no clutter. One font, consistent colors, and a single message. It's easy to read. It doesn't shout; it informs. And this commitment to quality doesn't stop at the mailbox. Their business cards, vehicle wraps, and even their team polos all match in quality and feel. Every piece adds to their credibility and tells the customer: we know what we're doing and we take it seriously.

Take Action Now:

Audit your print. Line up five things you've printed in the past year. Do they all look like they belong to the same brand? Are they clean and easy to read? Does the quality feel intentional?

If not, start trimming the fat. Keep it clear. Keep it consistent. And don't print on anything you wouldn't want a customer to touch.

Digital Drop: The Three-Second Test

Grab your most recent postcard, flyer, or business card. Set a timer for three seconds. Now look at it.

Ask yourself:

- Can you read the "what you do" part quickly and easily?

- Do you know what you're supposed to do next?

- Can you clearly identify who it's from?

If you can't answer all three in under three seconds, it's time for a redesign. Your customers aren't going to try harder than you did.

Rule #4: Know Exactly What You Want Them to Do

The point of print marketing isn't to be cute. It's to be clear.

Too many businesses waste money on beautiful brochures or clever postcards that forget the most important part: the call to action. You cannot assume your customer will know what to do next when it comes to getting started working together. You have to tell them. Directly.

If your flyer doesn't guide them toward something specific, you're just decorating the recycling bin.

This doesn't mean you need to beg for a sale on every piece. A call to action can be as simple as:

- "Schedule your spring tune-up today"

- "Visit our showroom to try it out"

- "Scan this QR code to grab your free guide"

Just make sure your print has one job — not five. When people are confused, they bail. Simple wins.

For Precision Comfort, when they send out seasonal postcards for HVAC tune-ups, the message is direct and timely. It's not "we do heating and cooling, yay!" It's "Get your furnace winter-ready. Book your service today." There's a single QR code that takes people to a booking page. Clean. Clear. No guessing.

Take Action Now:

Look at your last print piece. Is there a clear next step? One call to action? Or are you asking people to follow you, visit your website, call your office, and scan a QR code all at once?

Pick one goal. One step. Make it obvious.

Rule #5: Print Where Your People Are

Recently, I got a phone book delivered to my house.

Yes. Literal Yellow Pages with names, numbers, and the whole thing.

I was flabbergasted. I didn't even know they still made these.

Through my laughter, I opened it and started looking through the pages, then it all made sense. In between the A-Z directory listings was ad after ad for services like stair lifts, estate planning, flower delivery, home health care, and walk-in bathtubs.

You see my town sits on two ends of a spectrum: golden-era retirees and growing millennial families. The Yellow Pages were clearly after the silver tsunami crowd and missed the memo that while I say "back in my day" a lot more than I used to, a phone book isn't something that I need. But they blanketed my neighborhood like we were all jamming to golden oldies and clipping coupons.

The Yellow Pages know who they are marketing to. They know that for the intended audience, this marketing medium works. They know who uses the Yellow Pages and they placed their ads where those customers still look.

Print is not just about sending something out. It's about showing up with purpose. Whether you're placing an ad in the church bulletin, sponsoring the back of a T-shirt at a 5K, or dropping branded bookmarks at the library, think about where your customer's attention already lives.

Then print your logo there.

Take Action Now:

Make a list of five real places your ideal customer spends time. Not just online. Think about local hangouts, community events, schools, gyms, service groups, or places they already trust. Where would it make sense for your brand to appear? Start there. Then ask: can print help me show up in that space?

The Five Rules for Print That Works
(Quick Recap)

Real quick, lets recap these 5 rules:

1. Consistency Is Non-Negotiable
If your print doesn't match the rest of your brand, it confuses your audience and weakens trust.

2. Be Intentional, Not Accidental
Great print shows up in the right places, at the right times, with a clear purpose behind every piece.

3. Design Like You Mean It
Credible design builds confidence. Sloppy, outdated materials make people question your professionalism.

4. Know Exactly What You Want Them to Do
Every print piece needs one clear call to action: no guessing, no clutter, just guidance.

5. Show Up Where Your Audience Already Is
Your print should meet people where they are; in mailboxes, on fences, at local events, or even in phonebooks, not where you think it should be.

With these Five Rules you have the DNA for a powerful seed to PLANT for your business, but we need to add some digital fertilizer to amplify the success of your Print materials.

Digital Nurturing

Earlier we talked about how you tend your soil by having a nutrient packed website that we can plant our seeds into successfully. To add that extra fertilizer onto those plants, we integrate digital nurturing into our Print materials.

When it comes to print, the easiest way to add digital integration is with QR Codes.

QR Codes have been this wildly effective imagery that allows for people to avoid having to type all the characters and symbols that go into a website by just pointing their phone at them and being sent exactly where they need to go. When you rely on people typing in your company name or website into their browser you are adding another step that can slow them down to purchase from you.

Look at Amazon. When you go to buy whatever thing you ran out of or the thing your kid needs for school tomorrow, Amazon makes it really easy for you to buy: select your item > 1-click buy button > swipe right to left on their little slider bar > done!

Now because of this process, consumers want as few steps in their way to buy and so do you. The more steps, the sooner they can get distracted or talk themselves out of what you have to offer.

A QR Code is as simple as pulling out your phone > opening your camera > pointing it at the QR Code > hitting the button that shows up on the screen. This takes away any potential for fat fingering while typing, trying to spell out your business name, or trying to scroll through a list of potential brands that show up in Google.

The QR Codes takes you EXACTLY to where you want your customer to go and since you have this book, you know that each QR Code should have its own dedicated link that is tracked by your website analytics so you will know how many people scanned, visited, and did the thing you wanted them to do.

No more questioning or hoping. Just integration and tracking.

Now what?

Print Marketing is probably not how you expected to start our marketing belonging journey, but there is just something satisfying about holding a good print marketing piece. It lets you feel physically connected to a business even if you have never met or experienced them in real life.

Print shows a level of commitment, dedication, and investment in your business that many don't do.

In her over 30 years of printing logos and brands onto an infinite amount of products, swag, paper, and more, Sandie says there is one thing that never goes out of fashion or usefulness. It also happens to be the easiest way to get started with your Print Marketing journey: Business Cards.

Business cards go back hundreds of years, when people would leave their card with an important person's butler or doorman to convince said important person to talk to the business card giver. It was about sharing name, title, position, and address so they could know someone's position and have a way to write letters to communicate all manner of things.

Now business cards come in any manner of style, paper, color, and more. Marketing expert Jay Baer famously has a business card that doubles as a bottle opener. It is a useful, memorable, and surprising way to connect with someone. You will almost always forget or lose someone's regular ole business card, but a bottle opener? You aren't going to throw that out. More than likely you are going to put it in your kitchen and use it on the next bottle you need to open.

When you are putting your next print marketing piece together, think through the Five Rules For Print That Works and remember to:

- Get to the point
- Be on brand
- Have one call-to-action
- Add a trackable QR Code

Now, where can we use these fabulous print materials we are going to make? I am so glad you asked! Turn the page to find out.

Digital Drop:

As a woman, I am cursed with never having pockets on my most adorable and flattering clothes and I hate carrying a purse. So for years, I struggled with juggling not only my business cards but the one I was given. Then without fail they would get left somewhere, lost, or I would forget to follow-up with that person.

I stopped printing business cards and started using Popl for my digital business card. People just scan my QR Code (that is strategically placed on the Home Screen of my phone), they put in their contact information, they are automatically sent my information and I have set up an automation email so they get an "awesome to meet you" message that refreshes them on who I am and includes a link so we can schedule a 30-minutes networking call.

You can learn how to do this full digital business card system to streamline your networking in The Table community.

Get started with Popl at mrsdesireerose.com/popl

Your Takeaways

What were your takeaways from this chapter?

_____

_____

_____

_____

What real-world or in-person action will you take because of this chapter?

_____

_____

_____

_____

What digital action will you take to support or extend that effort?

_____

_____

_____

_____

Chapter 4: Networking

I've been an overachiever for as long as I can remember. Maybe it was my Marine Corps dad's discipline, maybe the "oldest-daughter energy," or maybe I was just born wired to do the most.

But no matter how many As I earned or clubs I joined, one piece of feedback showed up on every report card:

"Talks too much in class."

Guilty.

I've always loved talking with people. Hearing their stories, giving advice, problem-solving, or just being useful. As a teenage, I tied up our house phone for hours debating *NSYNC vs. Hanson, and I could turn any classroom into a mini networking event before the bell rang.

So when my mom sent me a link in 2009 to a site called Net-workingPhoenix.com and said, "Go meet people so you can sell your design services," I was already halfway out the door.

My first event was a "networking mastermind breakfast" (whatever that meant). I threw on my best business-casual outfit and walked in clueless. Tea in hand, I quickly learned everyone had to introduce themselves with something called an elevator pitch.

HUH?!

Somehow, I survived. That awkward morning set the entire course of my business life. My name has changed (#mar-riedlife), my pitch has evolved a hundred times, but that single breakfast taught me the most valuable lesson of my career:

Everything good in business starts with people.

Networking has been the heartbeat of every success I've had since. The smiles, the energy, the genuine care, it's humanity at its best.

These days, "peopleing" feels like a lost art. Social media gives us curated versions of connection: highlight reels, fil-ters, and hot takes. But in-person networking? No filter. No algorithm. Just people showing up, as they are, wanting to belong—if only for a moment.

So, in our post-COVID, overly-digital world, how do we bring that back?

This isn't a networking problem. It's a how-we-use-net-working problem. Networking didn't stop working. It just got stripped of intention, humanity, and patience. When networking turns into pitching, collecting cards, or chasing immediate ROI, it feels gross because it is. When it's practiced as relationship-building, presence, and contribution, it becomes one of the most reliable growth tools a business can have.

Proof That People Still Matter

If you want proof that showing up still works, look at Hartland Insurance in Livingston County.

The company has been part of the community since the early 1980s, when Barbara Walker bought the agency from her father. Today, Hartland Insurance is one of those names everyone in Michigan seems to know — not because of flashy ads or viral videos, but because they've mastered what I call boots-on-the-ground marketing.

They don't rely on algorithms. They rely on attendance.

If there's a chamber event, they're there. Ten of them, in fact. They belong to ten chambers of commerce across Michigan, multiple BNI groups, and nearly every local networking association in driving distance. They sponsor robotics teams, school programs, local festivals, charity drives, and parades. Their office is a revolving door of community connections.

But here's the part that matters most: it's not all on Barbara.

She built a company that belongs to the community, not just a person who does. Every producer, every team member, every representative is expected to be out there — shaking hands, building relationships, and representing the Hartland brand in person.

That's the real strategy. Barbara doesn't try to do everything herself. She built a culture of connection.

When your business becomes a familiar face at the ribbon cuttings, chamber breakfasts, and Friday-night football games, people remember you. Not because of what you sell, but because of who they see showing up. That's the kind of marketing no algorithm can replicate.

Hartland's marketing mix still includes billboards, radio, and TV, but those are just the amplifiers. The real engine is human presence. They've proven what so many businesses forget in the digital era: marketing doesn't start online — it starts with people talking about you in real life.

That's the modern twist on traditional marketing. The billboard gets attention, but it's the handshake that converts. The radio ad reminds them, but it's the chamber meeting that builds trust.

You can't just work from your home office and hope an opportunity finds you. As Hamilton says, "You have to be in the room where it happens."

The Networking Philosophy:
If You Want to Sell, You Have to Show Up

Networking is the original marketing channel. Before hashtags, algorithms, and perfectly timed email funnels, people grew their businesses by showing up, shaking hands, and talking to each other. It wasn't called "lead generation." It was called being part of the community.

Today, people overcomplicate it. They spend hours writing LinkedIn posts or trying to hack a social algorithm, but they'll avoid walking into a local chamber event because it feels "awkward." Spoiler alert: it's awkward for everyone. You're not there to be perfect; you're there to be present.

If you want to sell, you have to show up. Because connection always comes before conversion. Always.

1. Connection Before Conversion

When Chris Burns, co-owner of Watermark Restoration Services, launched his business, he didn't dump thousands into Google Ads or obsess over hashtags. He joined a BNI group. And then he did something most people don't have the patience for—he stayed.

Every week.

For a year.

Zero referrals.

My BNI: Preferred Professional Networkin Howell, Michigan

He still kept showing up. He listened, supported others' businesses, and focused on being useful. Because networking isn't a vending machine where you put in one conversation and get a sale back. It's farming. You plant seeds, nurture them, and wait for the roots to take hold.

When they finally did, they changed everything. Chris became the go-to guy for restoration in his community. He built deep partnerships with contractors, electricians, plumbers, and insurance agents. He grew his business to the point of hiring someone full-time to handle community marketing—attending events, sponsoring local causes, and continuing the cycle of connection.

Chris is proof that when you show up consistently, you don't need to chase leads. They start finding you.

2. Consistency Beats Convenience

Let's talk about Desi from Mayner Leadership for a minute. He's one of those people who leads with intention, but even he hit that "Do I really have time for this?" wall with BNI.

BNI isn't casual. It's early mornings, weekly meetings, required referrals, and accountability. Miss too many sessions, and you lose your seat. It's designed that way because belonging takes commitment.

Desi thought about quitting. The 7 AM meetings were a grind. Family mornings got interrupted. It felt like a lot for something that didn't always deliver instant results. But when he reviewed his revenue, he realized that a huge percentage of his clients came directly through that group. Not just one-offs—real, long-term relationships that grew from being known and trusted.

So he renewed his membership and doubled down. In fact, he didn't just stay—he became chapter president.

Consistency isn't glamorous, but it's the secret sauce of connection. Every time you show up, you remind people you're reliable. When you're consistently in the room, you become consistent in their minds.

3. Let People Taste What You're About

Back when I first started my business, I went to a women's networking event because it was free and there were snacks. A woman named Robi had just opened a luxury consignment shop called Urban Exchange in Scottsdale.

We got to talking about Facebook marketing (this was when Facebook was the wild frontier), and she asked if I could help. She became one of my first five clients.

Fifteen years later, she still calls me when she needs help.

That's the power of showing up and giving people a real taste of what you do. You don't have to give everything away, just enough for them to see your expertise, your heart, and your reliability.

When people get a genuine experience of what it's like to work with you—when they "taste it"—they'll want more.

4. Be Yourself Because That's Who People Connect With

Here's where most people overthink networking: they try too hard to sound impressive instead of interesting.

You don't have to "code-switch" your personality to fit the room. Be yourself. That's what people actually connect with.

For me, being myself looks like nerdy references, dry humor, and being a professional people person who's seen a lot of the world. I can talk Harry Potter with a Hufflepuff, chat about marketing strategy with a CEO, and share tomato plant woes with a fellow gardener.

These small details—your quirks, interests, and stories—are what make people remember you. Maybe you coach your kid's soccer team. Maybe you collect vinyl. Maybe you have a Mini Cooper that's basically your personality at this point. These are connection points.

People do business with people they like. So give them something to like.

When I talk about how I can't drink coffee but will happily down three cups of tea before noon, or how my container garden got decimated by deer, or that I'm convinced Slytherins just have excellent leadership instincts—it gets people laughing. It gets people talking. It gets them remembering.

Be real. Be a little weird. That's what makes you magnetic.

5. Bridge the Room to the Digital World

Networking isn't an end point. It's the beginning of your marketing ecosystem.

Every time you meet someone, think about how you'll stay connected after the handshake. That's where digital systems come in.

Start simple. Use Popl to capture contact info digitally. Add them into your CRM or email list—tools like Flowdesk or HubSpot make it easy to tag contacts by event or topic. Send a short follow-up email to thank them and share something useful. It's not about selling; it's about staying visible.

From there, build a nurturing sequence. Maybe it's a monthly newsletter or a short email series that shares helpful tips, blog posts, or new offers. The goal isn't to bombard people— it's to stay top of mind in a way that feels friendly, not forced.

The best part? Every conversation can fuel your content. The question you answered at a Chamber lunch can become a blog post. A story from a networking event can become a reel. If someone is asking for it in real life, others are searching for it online.

And once you've got those emails and content rolling, take it a step further—upload your CRM list into Meta or Google Ads to build lookalike audiences. That way, your marketing keeps finding more people like the ones who already know you.

It's not about replacing human connection; it's about amplifying it.

Digital Drop: The 5-Minute Follow-Up Rule

If it takes less than five minutes—send the email, tag the contact, make the note. Don't rely on memory to build relationships. Use systems so you can focus on the parts that only you can do: being human.

Find automation techniques at The Table.

mrsdesireerose.com/TheTable

Inside the PLANT system, networking lives in the "L" and the "T", the layers that build trust and long-term relationships that make every other channel work harder. It's where human connection gets planted so print, events, sponsorships, and digital marketing actually stick.

The Modern Networking Mindset

Networking isn't about collecting business cards. It's about collecting belonging.

It's showing up in the real world and backing it up in the digital one. It's how you move from "who are you?" to "I know someone who can help."

You don't have to network like a shark to succeed. You just have to network like a human who cares.

Because in business, just like in life, the people who keep showing up are the ones who keep growing.

So grab your name tag, refill your tea, and go be the person people remember for all the right reasons.

And here's the thing about showing up, it's contagious. Once you start, you'll find yourself craving more of it. More rooms where the energy buzzes. More conversations that spark ideas. More opportunities to bring people together instead of waiting to be invited.

That's where events come in.

Networking is the heartbeat of connection, but events are the body that moves it forward. They're the spaces where stories, ideas, and people collide in the best way possible.

Whether it's a coffee meetup, a workshop, or a full-blown community bash, events turn relationships into action.

You've already learned how to show up. Now it's time to learn how to host the room. Because the real magic happens when you stop waiting for connection and start creating it.

Your Takeaways

What were your takeaways from this chapter?

_____

_____

_____

_____

What real-world or in-person action will you take because of this chapter?

_____

_____

_____

_____

What digital action will you take to support or extend that effort?

_____

_____

_____

_____

Chapter 5:
Events

As a millennial woman, it's almost impossible to live in a small town without comparing it to Stars Hollow, Connecticut, the fictional coffee-fueled home of Gilmore Girls. With its quirky characters, charming town square, monthly festivals, and perfectly manicured streets, it's hard not to fantasize about grabbing a latte with your best friend and strolling arm in arm, gossiping about life in the middle of it all.

That's exactly the daydream Kathleen London carried with her every time she drove through the equally picturesque streets of Brighton, Michigan, on her way to her makeup shop, London Beauty.

From the day she opened her doors, Kathleen wanted to host a Gilmore Girls–themed event. She just couldn't quite figure out how to make it happen. So she started small. One night, she hosted a Gilmore Girls trivia game at her shop. That's where she met Laura Boote, a local content creator with a sharp wit and the same deep love for all things Stars Hollow.

The two became instant friends - the kind who traded memes over Instagram DMs and peppered their conversations with show references only true fans would catch. And the more they talked, the more the question kept popping up: Should we do this?

Finally, one day, they decided: Yes. We should.

Saying yes was the easy part. Pulling it off? That took months of late nights, color-coded whiteboards, and what can only be described as Gilmore Girls boot camp.

Kathleen and Laura knew they couldn't just tell downtown shop owners, "Hey, pretend you're Stars Hollow." Half of them had never even seen the show. So they created binders — actual step-by-step playbooks that laid everything out. Inside each one was a character assignment, episode clips, photos for inspiration, suggested decorations, even simple activities that matched the vibe.

If you ran the candy shop, congratulations — you were Taylor Doose, the town busybody. Own the diner? You were Luke. Antique shop? You were now Kim's Antiques. They made it impossible for anyone to fail.

And they didn't stop there. They hosted planning calls. They shared digital whiteboards. They answered every "Wait, who is Kirk again?" question with patience. Slowly, one by one, the businesses said yes. By the time fall rolled around, more than 40 of the 60+ downtown businesses had committed.

That in itself was a small miracle. Entrepreneurs are notoriously independent — that's why they're entrepreneurs. Getting that many small business owners to row in the same direction is almost unheard of. But Kathleen and Laura's vision was contagious. They weren't just asking people to decorate. They were inviting the town to step inside a story.

When the big day finally came, Brighton didn't just look different — it felt different. Overnight, Main Street had been transformed into Stars Hollow. A handmade sign at the entrance became the most popular photo op in town, with lines that stretched nearly an hour long. The candy shop was overrun with people eager to snap pictures with its new "mayor," and the shelves were stripped bare by the end of the afternoon. Some stores had to close the next day just to restock.

From morning to night, it was Disney World meets small-town Michigan. Families stood shoulder to shoulder in line for coffee, mother/daughter duos recreated their favorite Rory and Lorelai moments on the sidewalks, and women who had driven hours squealed when they spotted a Jeep that looked almost like Lorelai's.

Kathleen and Laura expected a few thousand people. They got nearly forty thousand. Shops sold out. Streets overflowed. Social media lit up.

But why? Why did a themed shopping day for a twenty-five-year-old TV show explode into one of the biggest events Brighton had ever seen?

The answer isn't just "because people love Gilmore Girls." It's bigger than that. It's about the moment we're living in:

40,000+ people attended Destination Stars Hollow.

A world that's gotten too digital, where we're desperate for face-to-face connection.

A hunger for communities built around really specific interests and niches, not generic networking mixers.

And a craving for thoughtful, quality experiences that feel curated instead of cookie-cutter.

Destination Stars Hollow wasn't successful because it was an event. It was successful because it became an experience that was thoughtful, intentional, and fun.

That's what so many people online get wrong. They think visibility is the same as success. They chase follower counts and views, but that's not what builds loyalty. People don't do business with you just because you popped up first. They do business with you because they trust you, believe you care, and know you'll solve their problem.

That's the connection. That's the "aha." And it's the blueprint for building a business that lasts.

Too Digital

Ever since COVID, our human behavior has been steered online. We went from being busy bodies with calendars full of plans to hermits who loved cancelled dinners and stretchy waistbands. At first, it felt like relief. But slowly, the novelty wore off. What was convenient started to feel isolating.

Now add the rapid acceleration of AI into our daily lives. Our work, our shopping, even our relationships are mediated by screens and algorithms. And while that technology isn't going anywhere, people are quietly rebelling. They're putting their phones down and craving connection again.

I know this firsthand. As an extrovert, COVID was brutal for my soul. I missed peopling — the casual conversations, the small-town events, even the awkward networking mixers. By the time 2025 rolled around, I made myself a promise: less scrolling, more showing up. I started using the local Facebook Events tab to hunt down in-person activities. That's how I found myself at a sourdough bread making class, knitting chunky blankets with strangers, and even learning to make cheese from a family farm. It wasn't just fun — it was nourishing.

And I'm not the only one. A 2024 Eventbrite survey found that 71% of Americans said attending in-person events is more important to them now than it was before the pandemic. People are realizing that the online world can't replace the energy of being together in real life.

That's the backdrop for why Destination Stars Hollow exploded. It wasn't just about Gilmore Girls nostalgia. It was about people who had been cooped up, screen-tired, and isolated for too long suddenly being given the chance to step outside and step into a story together.

Super Niche

The internet used to be about finding the biggest audience. Now, it is about finding your people.

When social media first exploded, everyone was shouting into the same crowded room. We measured success by follower counts and views. Over time, people stopped caring about how many and started caring about who. Who gets you. Who laughs at the same jokes. Who shares the same oddly specific interests.

We are living in the age of the micro-community. People are finding belonging in the hyper-specific corners of the internet. Thirty homeschooling moms on Instagram. BookTok fantasy smut girlies. Millennial dads who smoke meats and review coolers.

These are not broad audiences; they are tribes.

That is what Destination Stars Hollow tapped into. Gilmore Girls is not just a show. It is a language, a comfort, and a club with its own inside jokes. It is coffee at Luke's Diner, town meetings that never start on time, and the reminder that "where you lead, I will follow" is not just a theme song. It is a lifestyle.

Kathleen and Laura did not try to please everyone. They went all in on one community and built an experience for them. They knew their people would show up, and they did, with tote bags, flannels, and probably a caffeine buzz that would make Lorelai proud.

That specificity made it magnetic. When you create something that is unapologetically for a certain kind of person, that person will drive across states just to be part of it. They will bring friends, post about it, and turn it into a pilgrimage.

In a world obsessed with reach, niche is the new scale.

Quality Experience

You can tell when an event is being thrown together versus when it is being crafted.

After attending and speaking at dozens of conferences, summits, and networking events, I have learned that quality is obvious the moment you walk through the door. There is a big difference between an event that is a cash grab and one that is designed to create connection. You can feel it.

It is the difference between folding tables, watered-down coffee, and a room full of people aggressively swapping business cards, versus a space filled with thoughtful touches, intentional design, and meaningful details that make you feel seen.

The best events think about how people will experience them from start to finish. The signage is intentional and inspiring. The swag is useful, not junk that will end up in a drawer. The sponsors are thoughtfully chosen because they fit the audience, not just because they paid the highest fee. There are spaces for people to take photos, to connect, to rest, and to feel part of something special.

One of my favorite examples of this kind of care is the Women's Venture Summit in San Diego. It is a conference focused on helping women raise capital in a male-dominated world, but it feels more like a celebration than a grind. The event is stunningly designed, with clever touches everywhere you look. Pillows scattered around the lounge areas read things like "But first, invest" and "Have the audacity of a mediocre white man." The selfie stations are more than step-and-repeats — they are full installations that invite play and conversation.

Even the bathrooms are stocked with tampons, toothbrushes, and lotion. There are fresh flowers, infused water with lemon and cucumber, fruit snacks, and beautifully balanced catered lunches. The tote bags are high-quality canvas with sayings that make you smile. They even put stars on the floor for each speaker, giving everyone a little Hollywood moment.

And here is the best part: the schedule itself is designed with empathy. Sessions start late enough for you to have your morning coffee and end early enough for you to get your rest. It is a conference created for women who actually attend events, not just for the organizers' agenda.

That same kind of intentionality is what made Destination Stars Hollow in Brighton so magical. Kathleen and Laura made sure every business knew what to do and had the tools to do it well. Stores were renamed to match scenes from the show. The world's almost-largest pizza was made as a photo opportunity. The local bookstore became "Stars Hollow Books." They even thought about how to keep people entertained while standing in line. Everywhere you turned there was something clever, interactive, and fun.

These details matter. They are what transform an event from something you attend into something you remember.

In-person events of the future will not be about scale. They will be slower, more intentional, and built around thoughtful experiences that make people want to keep coming back. Whether you are hosting a major conference or a small-town pop-up, quality is what people talk about after the lights go off and the social posts stop.

How to Create Memorable Events
(and Make Them Work for You)

Let's talk about what actually makes an event memorable. Because it's not the free pens or the stack of business cards. It's the vibe.

When you walk into a space, you feel it before you even speak to anyone. A good event hums. The music, the lighting, the color, the people—it all pulls you in. There's energy. Someone greets you with a smile, there's laughter in the background, and maybe a cute little selfie spot that makes you want to take your phone out. You already know this is going to be fun.

Then there's the other kind of event. You know the one. A beige conference room with a folding table, a few wrinkled brochures, and someone half-turned in their chair scrolling on their phone. The coffee's lukewarm, and the room feels like a Monday. That's not connection—that's just attendance.

Memorable events don't happen by accident. They happen because someone thought through the details.

It starts with the vibe. Location, decor, and people set the tone. If you're hosting, make sure your space feels alive. Play music. Add color. Create a visual moment—a sign, backdrop, or prop that invites photos and conversation. Even if you're at someone else's event, bring that same energy to your space. Your booth, your table, your corner—whatever it is—should make people stop and say, "Oh, this looks fun."

Next, show up like you mean it. Your energy matters more than your setup. Don't sit behind your table with your back turned and a laptop open. Stand. Smile. Say hi first. Ask good questions. Look people in the eye. People can feel when you're just showing up to "work the booth" versus when you actually want to connect. Be the person who feels approachable, curious, and genuinely happy to be there.

Finally, leave them with something they'll remember. That might be something physical—a really well-designed handout, a high-quality giveaway, or a thoughtful little gift that ties into your brand. But it's also emotional. How did you make them feel when they talked to you? Did you make them laugh? Did you teach them something useful? Did you spark curiosity? That's what sticks.

This is where your print materials come back into play. Remember what we talked about in the print chapter? Those brochures, cards, and QR codes are not just paper—they're tools. Make sure what you hand people connects to what they actually care about. A beautifully designed one-sheet that says exactly what you do and why it matters will go a lot further than a generic flyer with a logo slapped on top.

And please, let's stop calling everything a "business expo." No one wants to go to a business expo. But they will go to a Home Trades Expo, a Women Who Build conference, or a "Taste of Local" showcase. Specificity is sexy. The clearer you are about what kind of experience people are walking into, the easier it is to attract the right crowd.

The Digital Bridge and the PLANT Framework

Inside the PLANT framework, events live in the "Attend" and "Nurture" layers. This is where your business shows up physically, builds familiarity, and creates shared experiences that digital tools can later support. Events are not a standalone tactic. They are the human touchpoint that makes every other part of the system work better.

Now, let's connect the dots. Because an amazing event that ends when everyone walks out the door is just a really expensive daydream. You need the digital bridge—that's how you turn the spark into growth.

Events are where we plant the seed. The digital system is where we nurture it.

Plan ahead.

Before the event, know your goals. Who do you want to meet? What do you want them to do next? Prep your materials, set up your QR codes, design your forms, and make sure your CRM or email platform is ready to collect leads.

Launch with intention.

Show up prepared and present. Capture photos and videos. Talk to people. Make connections. Have a clear reason for them to scan your code, join your list, or schedule a call.

Attract the right people.

Think of your event presence like a magnet. You don't need everyone—you need your people. The ones who will actually benefit from what you do. Your visuals, your language, your vibe—these are your filters.

Nurture after the fact.

Once the event wraps, the real work begins. Send personalized follow-ups. Thank them for stopping by. Share a recap or a photo gallery. Add them to your email list with a warm welcome sequence that continues the conversation. You're not chasing; you're caring.

Track everything.

Use your CRM or a simple spreadsheet to log who you met, where, and what next step you took. Did they visit your site? Schedule a consult? Buy something? Knowing the path helps you see what's working and what's not so you can keep improving.

Let's look at what this can actually look like.

When Mayner Leadership said they wanted to "meet strangers" (but the ones that would become clients), we looked at places and ways for him to have a physical presence with his target audience, home service professionals. We found a state level tradeshow for design and construction professionals for him to go to and we weren't just going to show up and hope people would stop by, we built a system.

His booth wasn't beige. It was bright red, branded, and buzzing with energy. He was out in front shaking hands, not hiding behind a table. He gave out high-quality pens that tradesmen would actually use, ran a giveaway for a free leadership audit, and followed up within forty-eight hours of the event.

Because he was a booth sponsor, he got access to the event's full contact list, so we created a dedicated email sequence to follow up with everyone—personal, warm, and specific. The people who engaged got moved into a longer nurture campaign that invited them into his coaching program. It was personal. It was trackable. It worked.

That's what an event looks like when you connect experience with the system. It's not about the size of your booth or how many people you meet. It's about showing up with intention, standing out with presence, and following up with purpose.

Now What?

If you take nothing else from this chapter, take this: people don't need more things to do. They need better reasons to show up.

We've all been to those events where you walk in, take one look around, and think, "Oh... this is it?" The vibe is flat. The lighting is bad. Someone forgot to put lids on the coffee. And you can practically hear the collective sound of everyone wondering when it's polite to leave.

That's not belonging. That's obligation.

What people want now is to feel like the event was made for them, that there was thought and care in every part of the experience. They want to feel something. Maybe it's excitement, curiosity, inspiration, or even just a sense of comfort that they're in the right room. That's the difference between people attending your event and people wanting to attend your event.

It doesn't matter if you're hosting something for customers, collaborating with your Chamber, or throwing a big community experience like Destination Stars Hollow, the goal is the same: Create moments that matter.

When you start building experiences that feel personal, everything changes. People show up ready, not resentful. They talk, share, take photos, and tell their friends. They linger a little longer.

They remember you because you gave them a story to tell.

You've now seen how the magic happens — how an idea turns into an experience, and how an experience turns into connection.

Before you move on, pause for a minute and ask yourself:

What's the vibe?

How do you want people to feel when they walk into your space, booth, or event? What story do you want them to tell afterward?

What's the value?

What are you giving people — physically or emotionally — that makes your event worth their time?

Who are you attracting?

Who is your version of the Stars Hollow crowd? Who are the people that would drive across town just to be part of your world?

How will you stay connected?

What does your digital bridge look like? Are you ready to follow up, nurture, and track the relationships you create?

What's your next move?

Pull out your calendar. Look at your Chamber events, community festivals, or industry gatherings coming up. Where can you host, participate, or partner in a way that feels intentional and on-brand?

You are not just showing up anymore — you are creating belonging.

Every handshake, every conversation, every selfie in front of your booth is a seed.

Your Takeaways

What were your takeaways from this chapter?

_____

_____

_____

_____

What real-world or in-person action will you take because of this chapter?

_____

_____

_____

_____

What digital action will you take to support or extend that effort?

_____

_____

_____

_____

Chapter 6: Sponsorships

As you drive east on I-96, heading toward Detroit from Livingston County, there's a moment when the trees open up and a bright blue billboard comes into view. A silver faucet juts out from the top corner, too big for the frame, pouring a steady stream of pouring water over one word: LOVE.

Below it, in crisp white letters, it reads: your water.

It's the Beauchamp Water Treatment Solutions billboard, and at night, that water droplet glows.

You might not think much of it at first. It's simple, clean, and confident. But in Michigan, that billboard means something.

This is the Great Lakes State, home to more than 20 percent of the world's fresh water. It's a place where water isn't just abundant; it's sacred. Michigan doesn't treat water like a commodity to be sold. It treats it as a protected natural resource, something to be shared, stewarded, and cared for.

Water shapes every part of life here. Summers are spent on lakes that stretch wider than horizons, where the phrase "heading up north" explains every Friday traffic jam. Winters bring lake-effect snow, the kind that blankets everything in quiet white and makes you grateful for the warmth of a home. Even the way people talk about weather, insurance, and lawns circles back to water: flooding, rainfall, frozen pipes.

So with all that water around us, why does a billboard telling us to love our water matter?

Because Beauchamp isn't selling us water. They're reminding us to protect it, to value it, and to trust the people who care for it.

And in business, that kind of trust is everything.

Beauchamp Water at one of their many event sponsorships.

Trust Not Transactions

Beauchamp built their business on trust, not transactions. In Livingston County, you can see the impact of that everywhere. Their name shows up at school fundraisers, veterans' dinners, Chamber breakfasts, 5Ks, and every warm-weather event where people gather. Their tents and coolers have become part of Michigan summers, as familiar as folding chairs and snow cones.

That presence did not come from buying ads. It came from participation.

Beauchamp understood early that you cannot buy belonging. You have to earn it. And you earn it by showing up with your time, your resources, and your consistency. That is what sponsorship looks like for them.

Sandy, their marketing coordinator, still laughs about how it all started. "We didn't have a budget," she said. "We had bottled water." So she used what they had. She joined every Chamber she could find and showed up with cases of water. For 5Ks, she brought hydration stations. For teacher appreciation events, she dropped off pallets. For veterans' groups, she loaded her truck and delivered what they needed.

It looked small at first, just another local business being neighborly. But people noticed. Their name became part of moments that mattered. A parent holding one of their bottles at a soccer game. A teacher grateful for donated drinks at a staff lunch. A veteran recognizing the same Beauchamp faces at the next fundraiser.

Little by little, trust formed.

Over time, those small acts became a system. Beauchamp added a sponsorship request form to their website. They tracked their donations. They aligned their giving with their core values of education, health, and community care. They treated sponsorship as a strategic investment in relationships, not a marketing line item.

That is how a small regional company became a household name in Southeast Michigan. When someone's water turns cloudy or smells off, they think of Beauchamp. Not because of billboards. Because of presence. Because of trust. Because they showed up.

Sponsorship made that possible. It turned their marketing into a network of relationships, not transactions. Great sponsorship does more than build visibility. It builds belonging.

Making Sponsorship Work for You

Sponsorship starts to work when you stop treating it like advertising and start treating it like participation. This is your chance to show your community what your business values, not just tell them.

Some sponsorships cost money. Others cost time. Many require both. All of them require intention.

There are simple, low-cost opportunities that still create recognition. Maybe you sponsor a local dance team and your reward is a small ad in their recital program and a poster where parents wait during rehearsals. It seems small, but those parents see your name every week. They connect your business with something their kids love.

You can contribute in-kind with your local Chamber or Rotary. Many rely on service-based sponsorships. If you help with design, photography, printing, or tech support, your expertise becomes its own form of sponsorship. These moments build credibility and goodwill without tapping the financial budget.

With more resources, you can show up in larger community spaces. Farmers markets, summer festivals, and town events like the Brighton Holiday Glow give you a chance to physically stand where your customers are. You get face-to-face connection, real conversations, and sometimes sales opportunities.

At Holiday Glow, for example, downtown Brighton turns into a Christmas village. Families gather, kids sip hot chocolate, Santa lights the tree, and businesses get to take part in the magic. This is not just visibility. It is emotional proximity. It is being present in a moment families will remember.

Some sponsors do not sell at all. They create memories. Lake Trust Credit Union did this with the Letters to Santa station. Kids wrote letters using their templates and mailed them in a bright red mailbox. Parents loved it. Kids remembered it. And while all of that was happening, Beauchamp was there too, passing out water to thirsty families.

This is the heart of sponsorship. It attaches your business to experiences people care about. Experiences build emotional recall far faster than any ad.

You do not need a huge budget to start. You need consistency, clarity, and willingness. Whether it is money, service, creativity, or presence, your contribution becomes part of the community fabric. That is how small businesses become known: not by shouting, but by showing up.

Sponsorship Is Your Brand Made Physical

Every business claims to care about its community. It shows up in mission statements, website footers, and networking introductions. But caring is not something you say. It is something you demonstrate.

Sponsorship is your brand made physical. It is your values, visible and undeniable. When you sponsor an event, you are saying, "We stand with this. We support this. We believe in this."

People notice who shows up for the things they care about.

Sponsorship sits in a unique place within your marketing ecosystem. It is not advertising and it is not charity. It is the overlap of brand, trust, and community participation. When you sponsor something meaningful, you place your business inside an experience that already holds emotional weight for your audience.

You are borrowing the trust that event already earned.

This is why sponsorship is such a powerful tool for small businesses. You cannot outspend big brands, but you can out-participate them. You can show up in the real spaces where people's lives happen. You can support their kids, their traditions, their fundraisers, their celebrations.

That is resonance, not reach.

When people remember your business because they remember a moment you helped create, that is branding in its purest form. It is how you become part of a family's memory. It is how you anchor your reputation in something emotional and real.

Sponsorship is not visibility. It is belonging. It is how your business stops being a bystander and becomes a participant in the life of your community. That is where trust is built. And trust is the foundation of growth.

The Sponsorship Spectrum

Sponsorship is rooted in community, but it is still a business decision. You are not sponsoring events because you want a gold star for kindness. You are doing it because your brand needs to grow, your visibility needs to rise, and your business needs to be in front of the people who will buy from you.

You can love your community and want to make money at the same time. That is the whole point of belonging-based marketing. Your involvement builds trust, and trust builds business.

The goal is not to be everywhere. The goal is to be intentional, aligned, and visible in the right places.

To help you make those decisions, it helps to understand the four types of sponsorships and what each one can do for your business.

1. Small and Simple Sponsorships

Low cost. High familiarity. Perfect for beginners.

These are the everyday sponsorships that keep your name circulating inside tight-knit communities without requiring a big budget.

Examples include:

- The local dance team recital program
- Elementary school yearbooks or events
- A poster in the window of a studio where parents wait
- Donating a basket for a silent auction
- Offering a small in-kind gift or service to help a fundraiser

These opportunities create micro-touchpoints. Parents, teachers, and families see your name repeatedly in trusted, emotional environments. Familiarity builds comfort. Comfort builds trust. And trust is the first step toward choosing you when they need what you offer.

Think of these as the roots of your sponsorship ecosystem. They keep you grounded and present in the day-to-day life of your community.

When to choose this:
You're working with a small budget
You want steady visibility
You're building early brand recognition
You want to get involved but don't know where to start

2. Community and Event Sponsorships

More visibility. More interaction. More opportunity.

These sponsorships put you physically into the community spaces where your audience spends their time.

Examples include:

- Farmers markets

- Summer festivals

- Holiday markets

- Local art fairs

- Concerts in the park

- Neighborhood celebrations

These events give you the chance to set up a booth, meet people, and even sell your products or services. You can connect face-to-face, hand out materials, answer questions, and put your brand into the flow of real community life.

At the Brighton Holiday Glow, for example, vendor booths turn small businesses into part of the Christmas experience. Parents shop. Kids explore. Families linger. And in the middle of all that magic, local businesses get to start real relationships.

These sponsorships are where brand awareness meets human interaction.

When to choose this:
You want both visibility and connection
You have something to demo, share, or sell
You want to gather leads or emails
Your brand benefits from real conversations

3. Experience-Based

Memorable. Creative. Emotional. Extremely sticky.

This type of sponsorship turns your brand into an activity or moment people remember.

Examples include:

- Letters to Santa stations
- Kids' crafts at festivals
- Hydration stations at races
- Photo op areas
- Games or giveaways
- Free treats or experiences

Lake Trust Credit Union nailed this with their Letters to Santa station. They were not selling anything. They were creating a memory. Parents loved it. Kids remembered it. And the brand became associated with a genuinely joyful moment.

These sponsorships are powerful because they attach your business to emotion, not just visibility. They build long-term brand recall and create a feeling people associate with your name.

When to choose this:

- You want to be unforgettable
- You want to stand out from other vendors
- You want to create social content or UGC
- You want deep emotional connection

4. Strategic and High-Visibility Sponsorships

Big impact. Big credibility. Consistent reinforcement.

These are your major sponsorships. They require more budget, but they offer significant visibility and authority.

Examples include:

- Naming rights (scoreboards, rooms, stages, seasonal events)
- Annual recurring sponsorships with Chambers or nonprofits
- High-school athletic partnerships
- Large-scale community initiatives
- Multi-event or year-long sponsorship packages

These are the sponsorships that say, "We are committed. We are stable. We are built into the fabric of this community."

Wayne Media, for example, sponsors the local Chamber as a media partner and handles their podcast recording. This gives them recurring visibility, backlinks, authority positioning, and steady community exposure. It is a sponsorship plus a demonstration of expertise.

These are credibility builders. Anchor points. Brand pillars.

When to choose this:

- You have an established budget
- You want year-round visibility
- You want to position your brand as a leader
- You're ready to deepen your community identity

Bringing It Together

Each sponsorship type serves a purpose

- Small sponsorships build recognition.
- Community sponsorships build connection.
- Experience-based sponsorships build emotion.
- Strategic sponsorships build authority.

Together, they create a layered, steady presence in your community.

Not noisy. Not pushy.

Just visible. Trustworthy. Familiar.

This is how small businesses grow.

By being part of the world their customers already live in.

Choosing the Right Sponsorships (Without Wasting Your Money)

Once you understand what sponsorship is, the next question becomes simple:

Which ones should you say yes to?

Because you cannot sponsor everything.

You should not sponsor everything.

And saying yes out of guilt or pressure is the fastest way to drain your budget and your energy.

Sponsorship works best when you choose the opportunities that match your audience, your brand values, and your business goals. This is not charity. This is strategy. You are building trust, but you are also building your business.

Here is how to choose what makes sense for you.

Start With Your Budget

A sponsorship budget does not have to be huge, but it should be intentional. Think of it like any other marketing line item. You want a number that is realistic and repeatable.

A simple starter model is:

Small businesses: five hundred to fifteen hundred per year

Growing businesses: fifteen hundred to five thousand

Community anchors: five thousand to twenty thousand or more

These are not rules. They are comfort zones. Every business is different, but having a number helps you say yes and no without emotion leading the way.

And remember: not every sponsorship is financial. You can contribute time, skills, product, services, or your presence. Many of the best sponsorships start that way.

Use the Sponsorship Fit Test

Before committing to anything, ask yourself five questions. If you cannot answer yes to at least three, it is probably not a good fit.

Does this reach my target customer?
You want alignment, not random visibility.

Does this represent my brand values?
You are tying your name to an experience. Choose one that reflects who you are.

Can I show up in a memorable way?
Visibility without participation rarely works.

Does this fit my budget?
If you are stretching too far, it will not be sustainable.

Will this help build trust or connection?
You want emotional proximity, not just logo placement.

If an opportunity passes this test, it is worth considering.

Choose Sponsorships You Can Participate In

The best sponsorships are the ones where you can actually be present. Booths, vendor tables, interactive stations, giveaways, or in-kind partnerships are all chances to talk to people and create connection.

If you cannot show up physically, make sure your presence still means something.

Examples:

- donating something useful
- supplying water, snacks, a resource, or expertise
- helping the organizers with something they need

Sandy taught us this. Her early sponsorships were not about money. They were about showing up with what they had. And over time, that consistency built a foundation people trusted.

Avoid the Common Sponsorship Traps

Saying yes out of guilt.
If you are supporting something only because you feel pressured, that is not sponsorship. That is people-pleasing.

Sponsoring events your customers never attend.
It might make you feel generous, but it will not grow your business.

Thinking your logo alone will do the work.
It never does. People remember people, not banners.

Not tracking anything.
You do not need a complex system. Just note what you sponsored, how much it cost, and what connections or opportunities came from it.

Trying to do everything.
You will burn out and your presence will be diluted.

Be choosy. Be thoughtful. Say yes to the opportunities that build the story you want your brand to tell.

Sponsorship Is Built on Alignment, Not Size

You do not need Beauchamp-level visibility to get real results. You need alignment. The right sponsorship, even a small one, can shape how your community sees you.

Families, parents, neighbors, and local residents remember the businesses that stand beside the things they love. Whether that is a dance recital, a fundraiser, a holiday festival, or a school event, your presence becomes part of their story.

Choose wisely, show up consistently, and your sponsorships will create the kind of trust no advertising campaign can match.

Digital Integration: Bringing Sponsorships Online

Sponsorships start in the real world, but their impact should not end there. The whole point of belonging-based marketing is that your offline and online efforts strengthen each other. When you show up physically, you gain trust. When you show up digitally, you amplify that trust and turn it into momentum.

The businesses that get the most out of sponsorships are the ones that treat every event like a digital opportunity as well as a community moment. You do not need complicated tools or a big team to do this. You just need a plan for what to do before, during, and after each sponsorship.

Before the Event

Create a simple landing page or website section specific to the event. It does not need to be fancy. Something like:

- yourdomain.com/eventname

- yourdomain.com/summermarket
- yourdomain.com/backtoschool

This gives you a clean place to send people you meet.

Add a QR code to your booth signage, flyers, giveaways, or even your water bottles. People will scan a QR code faster than they will type a URL, especially at busy events. Your QR should go to:

- your event landing page
- a lead magnet
- a discount code
- a newsletter signup
- a simple contact form

This is how you turn community engagement into a digital relationship.

If you have social media, mention that you are preparing for the event. People love behind the scenes content. Packing boxes, loading the car, building a Letters to Santa station, or setting up your booth can all become posts that warm up your audience.

During the Event

Take photos. Take short videos. Capture real moments. People love seeing themselves, their kids, and their community reflected back online. These photos become your content for the week and also deepen your visibility inside the event's own digital footprint.

Make it easy for people to find you on social. A simple sign that says: Come find us online with your handles listed clearly goes a long way.

Any time someone asks for more information, have a QR code ready. This saves you from handing out stacks of paper and keeps the conversation flowing.

If you are doing an activity-based sponsorship, like a craft table, water station, or giveaways, encourage people to take photos and tag you. You are not forcing anything. You are simply inviting participation. Most families will do it naturally.

Digital Drop: The High Value Giveaway

If you want guaranteed email or text signups from an event, run a giveaway that feels worth it.

People will happily trade their contact information for something fun, useful, or valuable. You do not need a giant prize. You just need something that feels good.

Great giveaway ideas:

- A one hundred dollar Amazon gift card

- A themed basket from local vendors

- A seasonal item people already want

- A gift card to a beloved local business

The bigger the event crowd, the bigger the giveaway can be.

Set out a simple QR code that says Enter to Win and send everyone to a short form where you collect:

- Name

- Email

- Phone (optional but encouraged)

One QR code. One form. A line of people signing up within minutes.

A good giveaway turns community pa rticipation into actual contacts you can follow up with later. It is the easiest, most reliable way to leave an event with real leads.

If you want templates and examples for event giveaway forms, you can grab them inside The Table.

After the Event

Your sponsorship is not complete when you pack up the booth. The follow up is where the magic happens.

Post a recap.
Thank the organizers.
Share pictures of the community.
Highlight the joy, the kids, the families, the volunteers, and the energy of the event. Lead with gratitude, not sales.

If you collected emails, send a simple thank you message. Include:

- photos from the event
- a link to your services or offerings

- a small discount or next-step CTA
- a reminder of where they saw you

This does not need to be a huge funnel. A warm, human follow up is enough to convert curiosity into connection.

Upload your event contacts (if you gathered any) into Meta or Google so you can gently retarget them. You are not stalking them. You are staying visible to the people who already met you and had a positive experience.

Repurpose your event photos and videos for the next few weeks. Each post extends the life of your sponsorship and reinforces your presence in the community.

Your Offline Effort Deserves an Online Echo

If you put time, money, and heart into showing up for your community, you deserve to stretch that effort beyond a single day. Digital integration is how you do that. It is not complicated. It is not technical. It is simply giving your sponsorship a second life online.

You showed up in the real world. Now let your digital presence carry that trust forward.

Sponsorship as Belonging in Motion

Sponsorships look different in every town, every industry, every season of business. Sometimes they show up as a booth on Main Street. Sometimes they are a water station at a 5K, a banner on a field, a donation to a school auction, or a station where kids write letters to Santa. The format changes. The impact does not.

At its core, sponsorship is simply your brand stepping into the real world and saying, "We care about this place and the people in it."

You cannot fake that.
You cannot shortcut it.
And you cannot automate it.

Sponsorships work because you are borrowing the trust that already exists inside the community experiences people love. When families remember the moment they saw Santa light the tree, or when runners recall grabbing water halfway through the race, your presence becomes part of a memory. That is a powerful form of marketing, because it is built on feelings, not funnels.

And yes, this matters for your business. This is not charity. This is strategy with heart.

You are not sponsoring events just to be nice. You are doing it because showing up consistently builds recognition, and recognition builds trust. And trust is the foundation of every sale you will ever make.

You are allowed to want both things: to support your community and grow your business.
That is not conflict. That is alignment.

A Light Touch of PLANT

Sponsorship sits primarily in Amplify. It is one of the clearest, most visible ways to put your brand in front of the right people in a way that feels good to them.

But it also supports the other stages:

- Prepare: Choosing events that match your values and your audience
- Nurture: Following up with the people you met using simple, human communication
- Track: Keeping an eye on what worked, what did not, and which events are worth repeating

Sponsorship is not a separate tactic living off to the side. It strengthens everything you are already doing.

The Real Lesson

Sponsorship is not about buying impressions.
It is not about slapping your logo everywhere.
It is not about trying to outspend competitors.

It is about participating in the life of your community with intention.

When you say yes to the right events, when you show up consistently, when you put your values into motion, people notice. They remember. They talk about you. And eventually they trust you with their business, not because you advertised at them, but because you belonged with them.

That is what makes sponsorship a cornerstone of belonging based marketing. It turns your brand from a business people have heard of into a presence they feel connected to.

And that is worth more than any billboard.

(And if you want a place to ask questions, plan your events with other business owners, or get guidance on what will actually work in your town, you will fit right in at The Table.)

Your Takeaways

What were your takeaways from this chapter?

_____

_____

_____

_____

What real-world or in-person action will you take because of this chapter?

_____

_____

_____

_____

What digital action will you take to support or extend that effort?

_____

_____

_____

_____

Chapter 7: Word-of-Mouth (aka Influencer Marketing)

Every town has one. It does not matter if your community has one stoplight or six roundabouts that confuse everyone who drives through. Somewhere on Facebook there is a group where your entire town gathers. The name changes from place to place, but the purpose never does. These groups are the online living rooms of our communities. They are where people go to belong.

Long before I moved to Brighton, I joined ours. I wanted to learn the rhythm of the town and see what mattered to the people who lived there. The very first day, I introduced myself in a welcome post. Within minutes, people were pointing me toward the best grocery stores, the quietest parks, and which pizza place was worth the wait. Before I even signed my mortgage paperwork, I had a new client. All because I stepped into a Facebook group early.

What I did not know then was that I had just joined the heartbeat of the entire area.

Our local group is run by a real estate agent who somehow ended up shepherding more than forty thousand neighbors. Forty thousand people coming together in one digital place. If you live anywhere near here, you are in that group. Your friends are in it. Your dentist is in it. Your kid's teacher is in it. Most of your town is in it.

And it is everything. It is helpful, chaotic, heartwarming, and dramatic, all in the same hour. One moment someone posts a breathtaking sunset over the lake or a photo of the deer that visit their backyard. Five minutes later the thread erupts into a spirited debate about potholes or school board decisions. Right after that, someone asks where to find a trustworthy roofer. Then someone else quietly shares that the food pantry at the park needs restocking and within the hour, it is overflowing again because the community showed up.

These groups are messy, but they are also generous. Loud, but also tender. Dramatic, but also deeply human.

This is why these Facebook groups matter. They are the digital extension of in-person community life. They fill the space between bumping into someone at the grocery store and seeing them at the farmers market on Saturday. They carry the tiny, daily moments of belonging that make a town feel like home.

And this is where the magic begins.

Because when someone posts, "Where can I get my knives sharpened" or "Does anyone know a great electrician," the comment section takes over. People flock to share their favorite businesses. They tag names. They tell stories. They give honest feedback. They jump in because helping each other is what this place is built for.

My certificate of completion as a CTA for my local community

Whether they realize it or not, every single person who comments is influencing a decision. They are shaping where someone goes, who someone hires, and what business gets chosen. In the ordinary act of responding to a neighbor, they become a local influencer.

Not in the polished, brand deal sense. In the real sense. The belonging sense.

In these groups, influence comes from trust. Influence comes from proximity. Influence comes from caring enough to help a neighbor solve a problem. It is grassroots, human, and completely unpolished. And yet, it works every time.

These Facebook groups reveal something important. Influence is not only something big creators do on large platforms. It is something communities do for each other every single day. The comment section is where local influence is born, shared, and multiplied.

And that is where we begin our deeper conversation.

Because as powerful as these groups are, they are only one piece of the puzzle. To understand influencer marketing and what it means for a local business, we need to zoom out and look at the bigger picture.

The Data That Explains the Problem

Most small business owners only see influencer marketing from the outside. They see teenagers dancing on TikTok or big-name creators holding up beauty products. They hear people talk about how powerful influencers are, but what they mostly feel is confusion. Does any of this actually work? And more importantly, does it matter for a local business?

This is where someone like Jim Louderback becomes important. Jim is one of the leading voices in the world of online influence. He helped build VidCon, the largest conference dedicated to online creators and digital culture. He has spent decades watching how people share opinions, build trust, and shape buying decisions online. He is not a trend chaser. He is someone who studies behavior. Someone who understands how attention moves.

Every week he writes a newsletter called Inside the Creator Economy, where he breaks down what is really happening behind the scenes. It is not flashy. It is not filled with buzzwords. It is simply an honest look at whether influence is actually working the way people think it is.

At the end of 2025, Jim shared something that made a lot of marketing leaders stop and pay attention. He talked about how influencer marketing, at the big national level, is starting to feel strained. Brands are spending more money than ever, yet the impact is slipping. Campaigns look good in presentations, but when they go live, the results are underwhelming. Audiences are scrolling past content that used to stop them in their tracks. Too many posts are feeling forced and recommendations feel transactional.

People can feel the difference immediately.

The IAB's Creator Economy Ad Spend Report mirrored that same concern. The spending keeps rising, but the confidence does not. Money is going in. Trust is not coming out.

For a small business owner, this is important because it explains something you have probably felt without having the words for it. People are becoming more skeptical of polished influencer content. They do not trust a stranger holding up a product as much as they trust someone who lives in their town saying, "This person is great! I have used them and they will take care of you."

The big influencer world is struggling not because influence has disappeared, but because authenticity has. People can tell when they are being sold to. They can tell when content is scripted. They can tell when the recommendation is not coming from a real relationship.

And that is exactly why local influence is so stinking powerful.

While national influencer campaigns lose their spark, local communities are doing what they have always done.

They are talking to each other.
They are recommending the businesses they love.
They are helping neighbors solve problems.
They are sharing their lived experiences.

These conversations are not polished or planned. They are natural. They are honest. They are rooted in belonging.

And that difference matters. Because when people trust the source, they trust the recommendation. Which means local influence can outperform big influence in ways that no data dashboard can fully measure.

The Power of Organized Local Influence

Explore Brighton Howell has become one of the strongest examples of how local influence can be intentional, organized, and rooted in community pride. They are our Convention and Visitors Bureau, but functionally they are something more. They are a hub where residents, visitors, and small businesses collide in the best possible way.

Their approach is simple: they spotlight what makes Livingston County worth paying attention to and make it easy for people to share those stories. Restaurants. Events. Trails. Shops. Festivals. All the things that bring life to a community. But the secret ingredient is how much of this visibility they hand over to the community itself.

They built a Certified Tourism Ambassador program that trains everyday residents in how to represent the area with knowledge, enthusiasm, and accuracy. It is not complicated. You take a short class, learn why tourism matters, understand how economic impact works on a local level, and walk away with tools that help you become a better storyteller for the place you call home.

More than four hundred people have gone through this program. That is four hundred micro-influencers working together without ever needing to call themselves influencers. They share their favorite spots, talk about their experiences, and lift up local businesses because they are proud of where they live. It feels organic because it is organic. Explore Brighton Howell simply created the structure that gave people a reason to show up.

This is marketing through belonging. It works because participation feels meaningful. When people feel connected to the success of their community, they share it. They talk about it. They bring others into it. Not because they were paid to post, but because they want their town to thrive.

For a small business owner, here is the lesson. You do not need celebrity endorsements to make an impact. You need people who understand your community and care enough to talk about it. Explore Brighton Howell shows what becomes possible when you invest in local voices instead of competing for national attention.

Local influence is not an accident. It can be nurtured, supported, and expanded when the right structure is in place.

So that is what organized local influence looks like. But influence has another shape too, one that is far more personal. To see that version, let me introduce you to someone who has become a familiar heartbeat in her neighborhood.

One Person, One Neighborhood, A Whole Lot of Influence

Local influence does not always happen at the citywide level. Sometimes it starts inside a single neighborhood, built by someone who simply shows up over and over again until everyone quietly starts relying on them. Every community has a few of these people. They are not famous. They are not chasing followers. They just care enough to stay involved, stay informed, and stay connected.

In the Brighton area, one of those people is Christel Meyer. Her influence sits inside the Oak Pointe neighborhood, a tight and highly engaged pocket of the larger community. And what makes her influential is not a platform. It is presence. Christel goes to the events. She supports local businesses. She shares what is happening around town because she genuinely loves being part of it all.

At some point, she realized that Oak Pointe needed a way to celebrate itself. The stories. The people. The small businesses. The unique moments that never make it to a citywide publication because they matter specifically to the neighborhood. So she launched Stroll Oak Pointe, a franchise neighborhood magazine designed to highlight the very best of hyper-local living.

The magazine gave her a vehicle to do what she was already doing naturally. By showing up, meeting people, staying plugged in, and paying attention, she knew the stories worth telling. She knew who had just launched a business. She knew what families were making an impact. She knew the new restaurant people were buzzing about. The magazine became a way to amplify the heartbeat of her neighborhood, not create one.

There is a difference between community and neighborhood.

Brighton is the community.
Oak Pointe is the neighborhood.

Community gives you a sense of place. Neighborhoods give you a sense of belonging. Christel leans into both. Her involvement with the Explore Brighton Howell CTA program expands her understanding of the broader area. Her work with Stroll Oak Pointe focuses that understanding into a

warm, close-knit circle where people see each other regularly and feel personally connected.

That combination makes her a trusted local influencer.
Not in the online sense, but in the neighbor sense. The real
sense. When Christel posts about a business, the people in
Oak Pointe pay attention. When she highlights a family, the
neighborhood feels a little more connected. When she shows
up at events, it reinforces her role as someone who helps
keep everyone informed.

She does not influence because she is performing.
She influences because she participates.

And for small business owners, that is the point worth circling.

Influence grows in the places where people feel seen.
Influence grows in the hands of people who show up consistently. Influence grows inside neighborhoods long before it
grows on the internet.

Christel is one example.
Your town has its own versions.

And your business can build meaningful visibility by connecting with the people who quietly hold the trust of the
neighborhoods around you.

How Your Businesses Can Tap Into Local Influence Authentically

By now you can see that local influence is not something en-
gineered in a marketing department. It is something people
build together without even realizing it. It grows in living

rooms, school gyms, farmers markets, and Facebook groups where neighbors trade recommendations and watch out for each other. It comes from regular people who care about their town and show up for it. Sometimes these people are loud about it. Most of the time they are not. They are simply present enough and connected enough that others begin to trust their voice.

The best part is that this kind of influence is available to every business, no matter how small. You do not have to be polished. You do not have to be perfect. You do not have to become an influencer the way the internet defines it. You just have to participate in the community you want to serve.

Local influence begins the moment people start recognizing you outside of what you sell. Maybe they see you at a fundraiser or standing in line for kettle corn at the fall festival. Maybe they remember you because you volunteered your space for a parent meetup or donated something quiet and helpful to the holiday drive. People file those moments away. Over time, they stop seeing you as a business and start seeing you as part of the life of the town.

That is how you become memorable.

Once you show up a few times, connections start forming. Every town has its connectors. The people who somehow know what is going on before everyone else does. The parents who sign up for everything. The residents who show up at every ribbon cutting. The folks who cannot help but recommend the places they love. These are not gatekeepers. These are your bridges. They love sharing. They love connecting. They love feeling helpful. And when you build a real relationship with them, they bring you into the stories they are already telling about their community.

This is where so many businesses accidentally mess things up. They assume influence is transactional, so they treat influential community members like marketing tools instead of people. That never works. The moment you turn a relationship into a pitch, the trust evaporates. What does work is simply letting people get to know you. Sharing your story. Inviting them to see what you do. Asking about their work with genuine interest. Supporting their efforts. Being human.

People talk about the businesses they feel connected to. They recommend the places that feel familiar. They share the experiences that feel real.

The digital spaces in your town make this even easier. Your local Facebook group is not a billboard. It is a town square. When you add value instead of noise, people notice. When you help someone solve a problem without angling for the sale, they remember you. When you show up as a resource, not a pitch, you earn a different kind of trust. One that makes recommendations happen naturally.

And if you want to become influential yourself, here is the secret no one tells you. It has nothing to do with creating more content. It has everything to do with creating more connection. Influence grows when you live in the community you are trying to reach. It grows when you post the photo of your kid at the pumpkin walk or celebrate the new coffee shop or cheer on the robotics team that made it to state. It grows when your name becomes familiar in the best possible way.

Digital Drop: Create a Local Referral Pod

You do not need a big audience to make an impact. You just need a small circle of people who agree to show up for each other when someone in your local Facebook group asks for help. When a resident posts looking for a service, your pod jumps in with genuine recommendations. No scripts. No spam. Just honest support.

My BNI group does this all the time. If someone asks for an electrician, several of us tag the same trusted person. It takes seconds, and it works because people notice patterns. They trust what their neighbors echo.

Your pod can be three people or ten. They can come from your networking group, your chamber, or simply fellow business owners you respect. The only requirement is integrity and participation.

Small action. Big ripple.

Local influence is earned through consistency and care. Not strategy. Not scripts. Not volume. It happens because you choose to be part of the place you serve.

When your business becomes woven into the rhythms of your community, you no longer have to chase attention.

The commnity carries your name for you.

The Part Nobody Tells You About Influence

Influence is not a trend. It is a signal. It tells you where your community pays attention and who they trust when they need help. Big brands try to manufacture influence with money, but local businesses do not need to buy it. You already live in the same ecosystem where trust is formed. You just need to understand how to participate in it with intention.

Everything in this chapter comes back to the same truth that has been woven through this book from the start. Belonging grows businesses. When people feel connected to you, they talk about you. When they talk about you, they bring others with them. Local influence is simply the community version of word of mouth, amplified by relationships and proximity.

This is also where PLANT begins to take shape in a new way. Influence does not exist in isolation. It grows in soil you prepare. It becomes stronger when you plant yourself in the places your customers already trust. It expands when you nurture relationships long before you need anything from them. Local influence is not something you chase. It is something you cultivate.

Your job is not to become an influencer. Your job is to participate in the belonging ecosystem that already surrounds your business. When you do that intentionally, people remember you. They recommend you. They see you as part of the community instead of a business competing inside it.

If you want an actionable next step, here it is. Choose one place where influence already lives in your area. Maybe it is your local Facebook group. Maybe it is a neighborhood pub-lication like Stroll. Maybe it is a community program like Explore Brighton Howell. Show up there. Contribute there. Become visible there in a way that feels human, helpful, and aligned with who you are.

When you do that, you stop marketing from the outside and start belonging from the inside. That is where influence hap-pens. That is where your business becomes part of the story your community tells about itself.

Belonging makes your business recognizable. What happens next is simply a matter of how far you want that recogni-tion to go.

Your Takeaways

What were your takeaways from this chapter?

_____

_____

_____

_____

What real-world or in-person action will you take because of this chapter?

_____

_____

_____

_____

What digital action will you take to support or extend that effort?

_____

_____

_____

_____

Chapter 8: Traditional Media

In 2003, when I was a college student, I unwrapped the gift that officially ended an era in my life: a pink iPod mini. Four gigabytes of freedom. Four gigabytes that fit in my pocket. Four gigabytes that meant I no longer had to time my mornings around a radio DJ who talked too long before hitting play on the songs I actually wanted to hear. With that tiny device, the world shifted. Music was no longer something you waited for. It was something you curated.

But before the iPod, I lived fully in the CD & radio era. And if you grew up anywhere near the time I did, you know exactly what that meant.

My first alarm clock was a little girl-talk radio alarm clock my mom gave me in first grade so she would not have to keep shaking me awake every morning. She set it to our local station, and that thing woke me up every day until I got my first cell phone in college. It was the metronome of my childhood. It told me when to get dressed. When to head to the bus stop. And most importantly, whether school was canceled for a snow day. If the radio said it, it was truth.

Radio threaded itself through every part of my youth. It played while I brushed my teeth before school. It filled the background while I did homework at the kitchen table. It blasted in the car when my friends and I piled in after practice, windows fogged from winter and teenage drama. It narrated everything.

And we all had that tape.

Sharing digital marketing tools with 9WGN Chicago.

A cheap, transparent plastic cassette filled with our favorite songs, recorded with dedication and hope. If you really wanted to show someone you liked them, you made them a mix tape with the best radio jams you could catch.

In 1997, mine was dedicated entirely to one song: MMMBop by Hanson.

I would sit by the speaker with one finger hovering over the record button, trying to cut out the DJ chatter that always crept into the first few seconds. I recorded the song over and over until I had an entire tape of nothing but MMMBop so I never had to rewind. Twelve years old, determined, and wildly loyal to a boy band. That tape was the closest thing I had to owning the song outright.

Radio was how I learned about new music. It was how I felt connected to the world before connection was something we could manufacture with an app. It was where breaking news landed with weight. It was a constant companion, whether I was a fourth grader waiting for a snow day or a high schooler waiting for the next band to soundtrack my life.

So yes, when I opened that pink iPod in 2003, everything changed. But the truth is, radio had already shaped me. It shaped my generation. It shaped how we experienced community, music, and each other.

And that is why, despite streaming, despite algorithms, despite everything we think has replaced traditional media, it still has power. Because it was never just about music. It was about belonging.

Local Broadcasting In Action

Local radio is easy to overlook until you see what happens when it shows up. And around here, WHMI shows up a lot.

I saw it for myself at a client's under new management re-launch. WHMI didn't just send a prerecorded message or plug the event from the studio. They walked in with equipment, set up a broadcast table near the entrance, and turned an ordinary business milestone into something the whole community could hear about in real time. They interviewed the owner. They highlighted what made the business special. They stayed long enough to turn that afternoon into an actual moment.

That was my first real glimpse of how WHMI operates: they participate. They put real people in real places to share real stories. For a small business, that kind of attention feels different from anything digital. It feels lived in.

And the more I worked with local businesses, the more I noticed the same pattern. A ribbon cutting, a nonprofit event, a seasonal festival, a new store opening. WHMI had a way of being there, microphone in hand, giving local stories a place to land.

It turns out this has been their rhythm for a long time. WHMI has been on the air since 1957 with their 372 foot tower in Howell sends a signal roughly thirty miles in every direction, wide enough to connect surrounding towns but focused enough to stay rooted in one community.

They are not trying to broadcast to the entire state. They are trying to serve the people inside that radius.

That is what makes WHMI such an interesting example of traditional media. They are not chasing algorithms or trending audio. They are not trying to be everywhere. They simply show up where life is happening in Livingston County. And when something matters locally, they make sure people hear about it.

It is easy to assume traditional media has faded into the background, but stations like WHMI remind you that some forms of connection never stop working. Not because they are nostalgic or flashy, but because they show up IRL.

Traditional Media, By The Numbers

It is easy to shrug off traditional media as outdated when you are staring at your phone all day. But if you zoom out and look at what people actually use and trust, the picture is very different.

Start with radio.

Even with Spotify, podcasts, and every streaming app on earth, AM/FM radio still reaches more adults each week than any other single medium. In late 2024, Nielsen reported that AM/FM radio reached about 213 million adults in the United States each week, more than live TV, social media on phones, or streaming video. Most of that listening still happens in the car, where local stations like WHMI sit right alongside playlists and Bluetooth.

Then look at local TV.

Surveys in 2024 and 2025 found that local TV news is still one of the most trusted places people go for information. In one study, nearly a third of adults said they see local TV news as the top source for unbiased reporting, above national broadcast and cable networks. Around 28 percent of Americans say they watch local TV news daily. Local late news in particular still delivers audiences in the millions, especially adults over 35, who also happen to hold most of the spending power in a household.

Print and local news are not gone either. They have changed shape.

Local newspapers and community publications now live in two worlds at once: print and digital. Studies show that people who are highly engaged with their local community and who vote consistently also tend to be heavy local news consumers. And while print ad spending has dropped, trust has not. Recent reports show that around 60 to 70 percent of consumers say they trust print ads more than digital ones, and that magazines and newspapers reach more than 70 percent of adults in the United States each month.

For small businesses, that trust matters more than the raw number of eyeballs.

People may not be reading the paper in the same way they did twenty years ago. They may be watching local TV on an app instead of on a cable box. They may listen to radio segments clipped and shared on social media instead of live in the car. But the source still carries weight. Local anchors, reporters, radio hosts, and bylines have something social media does not: a long track record of showing up in the same place, for the same community, day after day.

Traditional Media As A Distribution System

One thing that gets lost in the "traditional media is dead" conversation is how these outlets actually operate now.

Most local newsrooms are not thinking in either or terms. They are running a full distribution system.

When I worked as a social media producer for a CBS affiliate in Phoenix in 2013, I saw this up close. Inside the newsroom, no one was talking about social just for fun. They were very clear: the website kept the lights on. The website and the ads on it paid salaries. Social media existed to drive people back to that site, and the TV product existed to feed both.

We tested this with a local car wash during one of Arizona's big dust storms. Cobblestone Auto Spa offered free car washes if people posted a picture of their dirt covered cars and tagged both the station and the car wash. The promotion lived on social. It ran on the website. And it made its way into the lighter segments of the afternoon show and evening news.

One idea. Three channels. One big wave of attention.

That is how most traditional media works now. The TV segment is not just a segment. It becomes a clip on the website, a post on social, a link in a newsletter, and sometimes a short that lives on platforms like YouTube or Instagram. Newspapers and magazines do the same. The print story becomes a web article, a tweet, a Facebook post, and sometimes a paid boost.

Traditional media is no longer a single moment that happens once and disappears. It is a content engine that feeds the rest of your marketing if you know how to use it.

This is where traditional media fits inside the larger system. It strengthens credibility, widens reach, and gives your digital channels something meaningful to carry forward instead of empty noise.

Why This Matters For Small Businesses

Here is the shift that most small businesses need to make.

Traditional media is not "I went on TV and the phone rang off the hook" or "I ran one radio ad and sold out." That can happen, especially with national shows, but it is not the norm. Traditional media is about four things:

Proof of relevance.

A station, paper, or magazine chose you. You were selected, vetted, and given space. That alone signals that what you are doing matters.

Borrowed credibility.

When people see you on a local news segment, hear you on radio, or read about you in the paper, you are standing inside a brand they already trust. Their long term relationship with that outlet rubs off on you.

Reach into older and offline audiences.

Your boomers, Silent Generation, and a lot of Gen X still spend time with traditional media every day. They may also be on Facebook and streaming, but they have deep, habitual relationships with local stations and papers. Meeting them where they already are is just good manners and good marketing.

Content you can reuse.

A traditional media hit gives you video clips, screenshots, quotes, and links you can fold into your digital nurturing. Website, email list, social, Google Business Profile, sales decks, speaker reels, media pages. One appearance can feed months of content.

That is why even creators with millions of followers still light up when they get a segment on a morning show or a mention in a legacy outlet like Forbes or Entrepreneur. It does not necessarily get them more followers than a viral TikTok, but it changes how people see them. It is a status marker. A trust marker.

The same thing happens on a local level when your business is featured on WHMI, your city's CBS or NBC affiliate, or your local paper's homepage.

New Media, Same Human Need

Traditional media may build instant credibility, but new media gives people something just as powerful: time with you. And time creates trust.

The YouTube Chapter of My Life

I did not start on YouTube because I wanted to be a creator or because I had a grand plan to build a personal brand. I started out of necessity.

When my family received orders to move to South Korea, I needed a way to keep getting leads for my agency while living twelve time zones away from my clients. Networking events were gone. Local visibility was gone. Referrals were unpredictable. I needed something that worked no matter where I lived or what language was spoken outside my front door.

So I showed up on YouTube.

I taught what I knew. I talked about marketing for real businesses. I made videos answering the questions clients kept asking me. I figured if I could not be present physically, I could be present digitally in a way that helped people understand what I did and why it mattered.

What happened next changed my life.

By the time we moved back to the States, my YouTube channel had grown into a lead engine for my agency. When we bought our home in Michigan, the loan officer looked at my P&L and said I could qualify for the mortgage on my own. That moment blew me away, because it reflected years of work that happened on a platform most small businesses never think about using.

But here is the truth that matters more than the outcome:

I did not do anything fancy.
I did not have perfect gear.
I was not an influencer.

I just showed up consistently, talked like a human, and helped people solve their marketing problems.

And because YouTube is a place where spending ten minutes with someone feels normal, people got to know me. My voice. My teaching style. My personality. It was the long form trust that made the difference.

The Small Business Case for YouTube

YouTube is not TV.
And it is not social media in the fast, scrolling sense.

It sits in between. It is long enough for substance and casual enough for humanity. It is the modern extension of traditional media, a place where you can teach, explain, show, reassure, and guide without the pressure of being perfect.

Plenty of small businesses thrive on YouTube without ever going viral.

One great example is Brighton area realtor, Eric Meldrum who runs one of our local Facebook groups. Nearly all his clients come from YouTube. He films videos explaining what it is like to buy a home in Southeast Michigan, what different neighborhoods feel like, and what out of state buyers need to know before moving here. People discover his videos when they start researching the area, binge them, feel like they know him, and reach out when they are ready to buy.

He is not doing transitions or fancy edits.
He is simply helpful.
And helpful wins.

Small businesses are already having conversations all day long. YouTube is just a way to record the conversations you keep repeating and let people find them when they need them. You do not need perfect lighting or a ring light you bought at two in the morning. You just need clarity, consistency, and a willingness to show up as yourself, not the scared or over rehearsed version of yourself.

Podcasting: Radio's Cool Little Sister

If YouTube is the extension of TV, podcasting is radio's stylish little sister.

It is modern, flexible, low lift, and everywhere your customers already are: their cars, while cooking dinner, during commutes, while walking the dog, or while they are hiding from their kids in the laundry room. Podcasts slip into the quiet corners of someone's day in a way no other medium can.

They give you room to talk. Room to ramble. Room to share the parts of your expertise that never fit into a thirty second social clip. And unlike video, people are not nearly as afraid of sounding imperfect as they are of looking imperfect.

Most listeners are not expecting NPR level production. They just want a human who has something useful to say.

I know this because I have lived it.
I have hosted two podcasts.

The first, Marketing for Your Boring Business, featured some of the biggest names in marketing and gave everyday business owners a place to learn practical strategies. The second, Women of Video, ran for more than five years and more than 230 interviews, built with guests who logged on from all over the world, sometimes with nothing more than AirPods and sketchy Wi Fi. And it worked.

Because the point was never perfection. It was a connection.

And that is the magic of podcasting. It is the easiest, most accessible way to create long form content that can be repurposed everywhere: your website, your blog, your email list, your social clips, your YouTube channel. One conversation becomes a dozen assets without the production weight of video.

Podcasts Make It Stick

If podcasting is radio's cool little sister, then PR is the person who knows exactly when to bring her to the party. And no one understands that dance better than Lakesha Cole.

Before 2020, Lakesha was running a successful boutique clothing business. She started it while living overseas as a military spouse in Okinawa, Japan, building a brand that traveled with her every time the military moved her family. She created opportunity wherever she landed. She built community wherever she stood. She made it look effortless even when it absolutely was not.

And then, like so many small businesses, the world shifted under her feet. When the pandemic forced her to shut down her brick and mortar boutiques, she did not disappear. She pivoted. The very next day, she opened She Spark Media, her boutique PR agency.

It sounds dramatic only if you do not know her. Reinvention is not unusual for Lakesha. It is her native language.

She had studied journalism in college. She had worked inside newsrooms. She had interned at local TV stations. She had spent her whole life around media in one form or another. What she created with She Spark was not a backup plan. It was the culmination of everything she already knew how to do.

What makes her work so compelling is how she blends traditional media and podcasting like they were always meant to go together. She places clients on national and local TV. She gets them featured in magazines and newspapers. She shapes their stories so they show up as the most credible, powerful version of themselves. But she also treats podcasting as a strategic engine, not an afterthought.

To her, a podcast appearance is not simply a conversation. It is an asset.

She listens to shows deeply before pitching. She tailors each pitch to the voice of the host. She studies energy, audience alignment, editing style, and what makes a host say yes or no. She books interviews that have meaning, not just reach. And then she encourages her clients to reuse those moments: turning clips into ads, quotes into graphics, full interviews into long tail content that keeps working long after the episode goes live.

One of her clients booked 38 podcast interviews in four months and used those appearances to strengthen relationships with their top fifty retail partners. Another made 95,000 dollars in two days when the podcast clips were repurposed into targeted ads. She recently reflected that she and her team logged more than three hundred hours of podcast listening and research in a matter of weeks so they could pitch shows with intention, not noise.

Podcast booking is not glamorous. It is hours of research, relationship building, follow ups, and calendar coordination. It is patience. It is pattern recognition. It is knowing which stories land where. It is also knowing that influence often starts quietly, without fanfare, and then ripples outward when the right person hears the right story on the right day.

That is why podcasting and PR work so well together.

Traditional media gives you authority.
Podcasting gives you depth.
PR turns both into momentum.

A TV segment lands like a spotlight: bright, instant, public. A podcast episode lands like a conversation: intimate, thoughtful, long lasting. Together, they tell a fuller story of who you are, what you know, and why people should trust you.

And this is the overlooked truth for small businesses:

You do not have to be a celebrity to benefit from PR.
You do not need a bestseller.
You do not need a giant audience.

You need a story worth sharing and the willingness to tell it.

Lakesha's clients are not all household names. Many are small business owners, founders, makers, and service providers who simply want people to understand what they do and why it matters. Podcasting gives them room to explain. Traditional media gives them validation. And PR, done well, connects the dots so the whole story reaches the people who need to hear it.

This is the bridge between old and new media.
This is where belonging lives.

Traditional media says, "You are credible."
New media says, "You are human."
PR says, "Let me help people see both."

Before We Sign Off

Traditional media and new media are not opposites. They are different doorways into the same room. One gives you credibility. The other gives you connection. Together, they make you someone people recognize, trust, and want to learn more from.

You do not need a viral moment or a big budget to make this work. You just need to be findable, helpful, and willing to show up where your community already is.

If you want one clear next step, start here.

Reach out to your local media.

Look up your local newspaper, community magazine, or hometown news website. Every region has at least one. Many have several. Most are quietly looking for experts, events, stories, and people who can make their reporting stronger and more relevant. Your Chamber of Commerce can point you to the right contacts, and many Chambers maintain a media list specifically for member announcements.

Send a simple introduction.
Share what you do.
Offer yourself as a resource.

You are not pitching for a headline. You are opening a door.

When you connect with local media, three things happen at once:

- You increase your credibility,
- You widen your reach,
- And you create content that can live far beyond the moment.

This is how you start showing up in ways your community notices.
This is how you stop doing random acts of marketing and start building something that lasts.
This is how you move from being a business people stumble across to a name people recognize.

Traditional media puts your story in front of the community. New media lets the community spend time with you.

Both help you build the kind of belonging that turns awareness into trust and trust into growth.

Your Takeaways

What were your takeaways from this chapter?

_____

_____

_____

_____

What real-world or in-person action will you take because of this chapter?

_____

_____

_____

_____

What digital action will you take to support or extend that effort?

_____

_____

_____

_____

Chapter 9:
Digital to Human Marketing

There's a quiet assumption baked into modern business advice, especially in digital spaces. If your business lives online, your growth should live there too.

More content.
More views.
More subscribers.
More automation.

And to be clear, that assumption isn't wrong.

When digital marketing is working well, it does something incredibly powerful. It nurtures connection at scale. It allows people to find you, learn from you, and build familiarity with your voice, your values, and your perspective long before they ever reach out. Digital is where trust often begins.

I know this because I've built my entire career there.

Online is where I get to be a resource. It's where I teach. It's where I show up consistently. It's where people learn who I am not just as a marketer, but as a person. A woman. A mom. A military spouse. Someone a little sassy, a little gruff, and not overly polished. Those details matter. They're what help people feel like they know me, like they could sit on the couch with me and have a real conversation.

Digital is excellent at nurturing that kind of connection.

But nurturing and deepening are not the same thing.

There are parts of human connection that digital simply cannot replicate, no matter how good the content is. When you are in the same room as someone, your brain takes in information that never comes through a screen. How they sound. How they move. How they react. The pace of their speech. The energy they bring into a space. Even things we don't consciously name, like presence and warmth, create stronger neural connections. We remember people differently when we've experienced them in real life.

Online, connection is largely one-directional.

As a digital creator or business owner, you are giving. Teaching. Explaining. Performing, even in subtle ways. You exaggerate slightly so the message lands. You repeat yourself so it sticks. You show up as the version of yourself that works best through a screen.

In person, connection becomes two-way again.

That's where the relationship shifts.

You're no longer just the expert or the resource. You get to ask questions. You get to listen. You get to notice what someone needs, what excites them, what they care about. That exchange changes how people relate to you and how deeply they trust you.

This is not a digital marketing problem. It is a depth problem. Digital is not broken. Traditional marketing is not outdated. What breaks things is when businesses expect one channel to do the full job of relationship building on its own.

You see this everywhere if you start paying attention.

People will happily follow, watch, and learn from someone online for years. But when you look at how digital creators actually build lasting businesses, a pattern shows up.

They don't stay behind the screen.
They speak on stages.
They host meetups.
They fly to events.
They make time for real conversations.

Not because digital stopped working, but because showing up in person supports everything they've already built online. It gives context to the content. It deepens trust. It turns familiar faces on a screen into real relationships.

So What Does This Mean for Your Business?

If you're reading this and thinking, "That's interesting, but digital brands have nothing to do with me," I want you to sit with that reaction for a moment.

Because this chapter isn't here to convince you to become a content creator or turn your business into an online personality. It's here to show you how digital-first businesses are already doing something you can learn from.

The examples in this chapter focus on digital-first business owners, creators, and educators. Not because they're better. But because they've been forced to figure out how to nurture relationships at scale. And in doing so, they've uncovered something traditional businesses have always known.

You can't build trust in one place alone.

Traditional marketing practices like networking, events, print, sponsorships, and in-person presence are powerful. They create familiarity. They create recognition. They create real relationships. But on their own, they only go so far.

Digital marketing fills in the gaps.

It nurtures relationships between touchpoints. It reinforces credibility before someone ever meets you. It gives people context for who you are, what you believe, and how you work. By the time someone shows up to a chamber meeting, a local event, or your storefront, they don't feel like a stranger.

They feel like they already know you.

The digital-first businesses in this chapter are doing the same thing you're trying to do, just in reverse. They start online and bring their relationships into the real world. Traditional businesses often start in person and struggle to support those relationships digitally.

The direction is different.
The goal is the same.

A brand that feels cohesive.
A business people trust.
Relationships that last longer than a single interaction.

You don't need to abandon traditional marketing to build a strong digital brand. And you don't need to become digital-first to benefit from digital nurturing. What you need is alignment.

The stories that follow aren't about becoming something you're not. They're about seeing how digital and traditional support each other when they're designed to work together.

Once you see that, it becomes easier to spot where your own business could be stronger.

And that's where the value really is.

International Reach, Local Impact

I met Jessica in 2018 at Social Media Marketing World.

We were both at a TubeBuddy mixer, one of those events where everyone technically works online but shows up in person anyway. At the end of the night, people were peeling off in different directions, heading back to hotels. I had already ordered an Uber and mentioned it out loud, and Jessica and her friend Jackie asked if they could ride back with me since we were all staying at the same place.

That Uber ride changed more than either of us realized at the time.

Somewhere between getting in the car and pulling out of the parking lot, she asked me what I was doing on YouTube. I told her. She pulled out her phone, looked up my channel right there, and without missing a beat said something along the lines of, "Okay, you need to stop doing this, and you need to start doing this instead."

No fluff. No ego. Just sharp, honest feedback.

We kept talking after we got back to the hotel. Then we talked more. And more. I got to know her southern charm, her fiery redhead energy, her humor, her confidence, and her very strong opinions about what works and what doesn't. She was warm and blunt at the same time. Encouraging without sugarcoating. The kind of person who feels instantly familiar.

We became friends right then and there.

Jessica built her business online because she wanted to stay home with her boys. That was the driving force. She didn't set out to build a massive personal brand or chase internet fame. She wanted a digital business that gave her flexibility, income, and control over her time.

And she worked for it.

Her business didn't come together easily or quickly. There were pivots. Struggles. Periods where things felt heavy and uncertain. But she kept showing up. She built digital products. She built an audience. She built trust. Over time, her reach stretched far beyond the small town she lived in. Her brand became international.

That digital brand is the foundation of everything she does.

But what's most interesting about Jessica isn't just the size of her audience or the success of her online business. It's how intentionally she chose to apply that success closer to home.

Jessica lives in a small southern town built around tourism, small businesses, and one big company everyone wants to work for. Like a lot of small towns, there was pride there, but also hesitation around digital marketing and modern branding. At first, her success online didn't automatically translate to local support. In some ways, it created distance.

Until local business owners started reaching out.

Quietly at first. Messages asking questions. DMs asking for help. Business owners who had watched her grow online and realized she understood something they didn't. They weren't asking her to turn them into internet brands. They wanted help supporting the businesses they already had.

That's when Jessica built a small, boutique agency alongside her digital brand.

Not to scale endlessly. Not to serve everyone. But to serve her community.

Her agency supports a limited number of local businesses who benefit directly from her digital expertise. Tourism-based businesses. Independent shops. Local brands that need visibility beyond foot traffic and seasonal spikes. She helps them think differently about how people find them, how their stories are told, and how digital tools can support real-world sales.

Her digital business gives her leverage.

Her local agency gives her impact.

She didn't choose one or the other. She let them support each other.

The international reach of her digital brand established authority. The local application of that knowledge made it tangible.

That's the pattern digital businesses often miss.

You don't have to abandon what you've built online to make an impact in real life. You can use your digital credibility to support a smaller, more intentional, in-person arm of your business that deepens trust and strengthens the community you want to be part of.

Jessica didn't leave the internet. She let it enhance her local life and business.

The Biggest Digital Launch Ever Was Marketed With Mail

Alex Hormozi is one of the biggest names in modern digital marketing. His businesses are built almost entirely online. His frameworks are taught at massive scale. His content reaches millions. He operates in a world of systems, leverage, and efficiency.

Which is exactly why his choice to use physical mail stands out.

I've read his books and followed his work, like a lot of business owners who want to keep up with the digital Joneses. When he launched his massive campaign for his third book, 100M Money Models, I didn't just see it online. I saw it in my mailbox.

A real piece of mail.
Sent through the post office.
Delivered to my house.

Inside was an actual letter about a digital launch and a live online event.

At first glance, it feels almost ironic. One of the most digitally sophisticated marketers in the world choosing one of the most analog channels available. But when you look at it through the lens of relationship depth instead of reach, it makes perfect sense.

Online, Hormozi already had my attention.
Offline, he earned my pause.

That piece of mail did something his content didn't need to do. It didn't explain who he was or what he offered. It simply reinforced the relationship. It created a moment that lived outside the feed, outside the inbox, outside the constant scroll.

And that is the in-real-life equivalent of being scroll-stopping.

Especially when you consider that mail is expensive. Mail takes effort. Mail is intentional.

Hormozi didn't need it to succeed. His launch would have done well without it. But at his level of scale, attention is fragmented and audiences are flooded with content. Physical touchpoints cut through because they show up where digital noise can't.

At Hormozi's scale, digital already does what it's supposed to do.

His content educates. His systems convert. His audience is deeply engaged. The internet wasn't the weak point in this launch. It was the foundation.

And the results prove it.

That book launch went on to sell over three million copies in three days, generated over one hundred million dollars, and set a Guinness World Record for the fastest-selling non-fiction book in twenty-four hours. A book about digital business and digital models became one of the biggest publishing successes ever recorded.

And part of how it was supported was with good old-fashioned snail mail.

That's not irony. That's strategy.

When digital does the nurturing, print can do the grounding. It slows people down long enough to pay attention and reminds them there's a real operation behind the screen.

Hormozi didn't use mail because digital marketing failed. He used it because digital marketing worked, and this made it stronger.

And when a digital marketing book sets a Guinness World Record with help from the post office, it's worth paying attention to.

Creators Who Built the Room They Wanted to Be In

Colin and Samir are one of the most respected duos in the creator education space, and their business was built almost entirely online.

They started scrappy. Before the podcast, before the millions of subscribers, before the brand deals, they were experimenting on the internet, trying to figure out how to build something sustainable by creating content people actually cared about. Eventually, they found their lane by doing something deceptively simple: interviewing other creators about how they built their businesses.

Their podcast and YouTube channel became required listening for anyone serious about the creator economy. They didn't just talk about tactics. They talked about careers, tradeoffs, money, burnout, leverage, and longevity. Over time, that approach helped them grow an audience of over a million subscribers.

One of their most iconic moments happened live on stage at VidSummit, when they watched their subscriber count cross one million in real time. A digital milestone, reached in a physical room, surrounded by the very people who helped make it happen.

They were already winning online.

They were invited to speak at every major creator economy event. VidSummit. VidCon. Industry conferences. Brand events. Panels. Keynotes. They were everywhere.

And yet, something still felt missing.

They talk openly about this now, but at the time, it showed up as a quiet frustration. They were participating in the creator economy, but not always in a way that felt aligned. The rooms they were invited into didn't always reflect the kinds of conversations they wanted to have or the depth their audience was craving.

So instead of trying to fit better into existing events, they did something different.

They built their own.

Colin & Samir at their first in-person event, Sept 2025.

Publish Press NYC wasn't designed to scale endlessly. It wasn't meant to be the biggest creator event in the world. It was intentionally small. Around four hundred people. Application required. Paid tickets. One day.

Every choice was deliberate.

The event mirrored their digital brand. Conversation-driven. Interview-focused. Creator-first. They brought together creators and brands like YouTube and Spotify, alongside voices like Casey Neistat and Steven Bartlett. Not to lecture, but to talk. To share real experiences. To let people learn by listening in on conversations they normally wouldn't have access to.

What made the event work wasn't production value or hype. It was alignment.

You could feel the buy-in in the room because the people there already trusted Colin and Samir online. The event didn't introduce them. It deepened the relationship. It took a digital audience and gave it a shared, in-person experience.

That's the move digital creators often overlook.

Events aren't just about monetization or visibility. They're about compression. They take years of online trust and condense it into a single day. They turn passive consumption into active participation. They create memories that live longer than a piece of content ever will.

Colin and Samir didn't build an event because digital stopped working for them.
They built it because digital worked so well that people wanted to be in the same room.

And instead of renting space in someone else's vision, they created a space that reflected their own.

So What Can You Actually Do?

If you're a local business owner, a chamber member, or someone whose business is rooted in a real community, this isn't about copying what Jessica, Hormozi, or Colin and Samir did.

It's about understanding what they paid attention to.

Each of them asked a version of the same question: how do I deepen the relationships I'm already building?

For a business like yours, that question usually starts closer to home than you think. You're already showing up in rooms. You're already meeting people face to face. You're already building relationships that begin with a conversation, a referral, or a handshake.

The opportunity isn't to add more activity. It's to make sure those moments don't end when the event does.

That often means looking at how your digital presence supports what's happening in real life. When someone looks you up after a chamber meeting or local event, do they recognize the person they just talked to? Does your website, your content, or your email presence reflect the same clarity and confidence they experienced in person?

It can also mean using digital tools to stay connected between in-person touchpoints. Sharing useful information. Highlighting partnerships. Showing up consistently enough that people remember you between meetings, not just at them.

In some cases, it means adding a physical or in-person element that reinforces your digital work. A printed piece. A mailed thank-you. A hosted gathering. Something tangible that signals effort and intention without needing to be elaborate.

The goal isn't to become louder or more visible for the sake of it. It's to become more familiar.

The businesses in this chapter didn't treat digital and traditional marketing as separate strategies. They let each one do what it does best. Digital nurtured the relationship. In-person interaction deepened it.

When those two things work together, marketing stops feeling scattered. Your online presence supports your real-world reputation. Conversations move faster because trust is already there. Referrals happen more naturally because people know how to talk about what you do.

You don't need a massive audience. You don't need to go viral. And you don't need to do everything.

You just need to make sure the way people experience you online supports the way they experience you in real life.

That's how digital branding strengthens traditional businesses. And that's how traditional businesses stop leaving opportunity on the table.

That's where it all comes together.

Inside the PLANT system, this chapter lives at the intersection. Digital is the nurture layer that supports everything else you are already doing. It keeps relationships warm between networking meetings, events, sponsorships, and print moments, so trust does not reset every time you leave the room.

Digital Drop: The Three-Question Digital Check

This chapter is about how digital businesses use in-person connection to deepen relationships, and how traditional businesses can strengthen what they're already doing by using digital more intentionally.

Before you move on, take a moment to do a quick digital check. This isn't a full audit and it's not about fixing anything yet. It's simply about noticing how your digital presence is supporting, or not supporting, the relationships you're building in real life.

Answer these three questions:

Where do people most often meet you in person? What do they see when they look you up afterward? Does what they see digitally support the conversation you just had in person?

Once you've answered these for yourself, take your reflections into The Table. Share what stood out, what felt aligned, or where things felt disconnected. Seeing how other business owners answer these questions often brings clarity you wouldn't get on your own.

Your Takeaways

What were your takeaways from this chapter?

_____

_____

_____

_____

What real-world or in-person action will you take because of this chapter?

_____

_____

_____

_____

What digital action will you take to support or extend that effort?

_____

_____

_____

_____

Chapter 10:
Belonging Is the Work That Lasts

When I speak on stages about marketing, I've often used a Lord of the Rings analogy. I've said that businesses should act like Gandalf, guiding their customers, Frodo, through the journey to the final outcome.

And honestly? I don't think that analogy holds up anymore.

Because if we're being real, you are not Gandalf. You never were.

You're Frodo.

You're the one carrying the heavy load. You're the one doing the hard, often invisible work. You're the one solving real problems so that the people you serve can keep living their lives with a little more ease, stability, and peace. Your customers aren't Frodo. They're the Shire. They're what you're protecting. They get to benefit from the journey without having to walk every brutal mile themselves.

Gandalf shows up, sets the quest in motion, and then goes and does his own thing. That's not what most business owners need, and it's certainly not what I want to be for you.

If anything, the role that actually matters is Samwise Gamgee.

Sam isn't in it for glory. He's not chasing credit. He doesn't pretend the journey is easy. He just stays. He carries the load when it's too heavy. He reminds Frodo who he is when the road starts to break him down. He believes in the mission even when it feels impossible.

That's the role I want this book to play on your journey.

Not a grand speech. Not a magic solution. But a steady companion. Something you can come back to when the terrain feels confusing, when marketing feels heavier than it should, and when you need to be reminded that you're not failing, you're just in the middle of something hard.

And yes, Sam also happens to be a gardener. Someone who understands that growth doesn't come from force or shortcuts, but from care, patience, and tending what matters over time. That is what he does for Frodo by continuing to show up, giving him the foundation and support he needs to make it through rocky terrain, scary monsters, and tempting distractions.

And when the journey finally ends, the story doesn't pretend everything is suddenly easy. It simply acknowledges this: the work mattered, the weight was real, and the path forward is clearer because of what was carried and learned along the way.

That's where we are now.

Now, stepping out of the story and back into the real world, here's what I want you to hold onto.

Marketing works best when it stops being a collection of disconnected tasks and starts being a reflection of how you actually show up in the world. The reason the strategies in this book work isn't because they're flashy or new. It's because they reinforce each other. They create familiarity. They build trust. They give people multiple, consistent ways to know you and remember you.

You don't need to do everything in this book at once. You were never meant to. What matters is that whatever you choose to do, you do it with intention and consistency. One clear message, repeated in the right places, over time, will always outperform scattered effort.

If marketing has felt overwhelming in the past, it's not because you couldn't handle it. It's because you were trying to carry too much without a system that made sense. Now you have one. Not a rigid plan, but a way of thinking that lets you decide what fits and what doesn't.

From here on out, your job isn't to chase every new idea. It's to notice when something aligns with how you want to serve people and when it doesn't. It's to choose clarity over noise, relationships over reach, and belonging over burnout.

This book doesn't end your work. It sharpens it.

You're still building. You're still learning. You're still in motion. But now, you're doing it with a clearer sense of what matters and a steadier way to move forward.

That's enough.

When you strip everything else away, this book comes down to one idea.

Belonging.

Not as a buzzword. Not as a campaign. Not as something you manufacture or force. Belonging is what happens when people experience you enough times, in enough ways, to trust that you're here and you're not going anywhere.

That's why the strategies in this book work. They aren't designed to grab attention once. They're designed to create familiarity over time. To help people recognize you, remember you, and feel comfortable coming back.

Belonging doesn't require you to be everywhere. It requires you to be consistent. It doesn't ask you to perform. It asks you to show up as yourself, clearly and reliably.

When your marketing is built around belonging, it stops feeling like something you have to keep up with and starts feeling like an extension of how you already serve people. The pressure eases. The noise fades. Decisions get simpler.

From here on out, you don't need to ask, "What should I post?" or "What am I missing?" The better question is, "Does this help someone feel more connected to me, my work, or the community I serve?"

If the answer is yes, you're on the right path.

This book doesn't give you a finish line, because belonging isn't something you complete. It's something you practice. Quietly. Consistently. Over time.

Your garden is ready. Stop marketing. Start belonging.

About The Author

Desiree Martinez has been marketing since Myspace, back when coding your profile was the ultimate flex. With more than 15 years of experience helping small businesses grow, she has built a career turning marketing overwhelm into clarity and connection. As the founder and CEO of The Kast Agency, Desiree helps service-based and community-driven businesses build strategies that actually work in the real world.

Known for her straightforward, sassy approach, Desiree has partnered with brands like Adobe, Streamyard, and VidIQ, and has helped thousands of small business owners grow through trust, consistency, and community.

When she is not coaching or creating content, Desiree can be found on her Michigan homestead, sipping tea, rolling dice in Dungeons & Dragons, or chasing her next big idea.

Stop Marketing, Start Belonging is her guide for building loyal customers and a business people truly care about.

THE TABLE

The Table is where this book turns into action.

It is an online space for business owners who want clear, practical marketing support without chasing trends or doing everything alone.

Inside The Table, you get:

- Step-by-step tutorials for both digital and traditional marketing
- Clear instructions you can actually follow, not theory
- Weekly office hours to ask questions and work through challenges
- Ongoing support as you implement, not after the fact
- A community of business owners navigating the same decisions you are

This is not about doing more marketing. It is about doing the right things, in the right order, with support.

If you want help putting what you are reading into practice and staying consistent without overwhelm, The Table gives you a place to do that, all in one spot, online and on your schedule.

Learn more or join at: mrsdesireerose.com/TheTable

Real People. Real Businesses.

Every person, business, and example referenced in this book is real.

The stories shared here are not composites or hypothetical case studies. They are drawn from real businesses, real communities, and real people who were actively building connection and belonging at the time this book was written.

Because businesses evolve, g row, change ownership, or shift direction over time, I've created a dedicated page where you can learn more about the people and companies mentioned, directly from their own platforms.

First Impressions Print and Marketing Sandie Cortez https://firstimpressionsprint.com	Inside the Creator Economy Jim Louderback https://www.creatoreconomyshow.com	Watermark Restoration Services Chris Burns https://watermarkrestoration.com
Precision Comfort Heating and Air Conditioning Leadership team referenced https://www.precisioncomfort.com	Stroll Oak Point Christel Meyer https://www.strollmag.com/locations/oak-pointe-mi/	Hartland Insurance Barbara Walker https://www.hartlandinsurance.com
Mayner Leadership Desi Mayner https://maynerleadership.com	WHMI Radio Local media organization referenced https://www.whmi.com	Real Estate One Tina Peterson https://www.tinapetersonteam.com/

Urban Exchange (Scottsdale) Business owners and local vendors referenced https://urbanexchang-escottsdale.com	Tru Living Group, eXp Realty Eric Meldrum https://www.truliv-inggroup.com	Explore Brighton Howell Community media brand referenced https://explorebrigh-tonhowell.com
London Beauty Business owner referenced Website not publicly listed at time of writing	She Spark Media Lakesha Cole https://shes-parkmedia.com	Howell Chamber of Commerce Janelle Smith, President https://www.howell-chamber.com
Women's Venture Summit Event organization referenced https://womensven-turesummit.com	Away Home MI Chris Burns https:// awayhomemi.com	Jessica Stansberry Creator and educator referenced https://jessicast-ansberry.com
Brighton Holiday Glow (Brighton Chamber of Commerce) Brighton Area Chamber of Commerce https://www.brightoncoc.org	Beauchamp Water Treatment Solutions Beauchamp family leadership team https://www.beau-champwater.com	Business Network International (BNI) Chapter-based global organization https://www.bni.com
Alex Hormozi Entrepreneur and author referenced https://www.ac-quisition.com	Colin & Samir Colin Rosenblum and Samir Chaudry https://www.co-linandsamir.com	Rotary International Local Rotary chapters referenced https://www.rotary.org

Sources and References

Throughout this book, I reference research, reports, and industry data to support the ideas, examples, and strategies shared. Rather than crowd the pages with footnotes or interrupt the flow of the stories, I've gathered all referenced sources in one place online.

You can view the full, up-to-date list of sources referenced in this book at:

mrsdesireerose.com/BookSources

This page includes direct links to studies, reports, and organizations covering topics like media trust, word-of-mouth marketing, traditional advertising, digital behavior, and community-driven growth.

If you're someone who likes to dig deeper, verify data, or explore the research behind the strategies in this book, that page is there for you.

And if you're not, that's okay too. This book was written to be practical first. The sources simply support what many business owners already know from experience.

Belonging works.

www.ingramcontent.com/pod-product-compliance
Lightning Source LLC
Chambersburg PA
CBHW071607210326
41597CB00019B/3439